COVID CHRONICLES

The Secret Diary of a Lazy Cow in Lockdown

www.davidtristram.uk

well wishers

Raising funds to make a difference

Even though laughter is generally the best medicine, there may be times when we need a little extra specialist help.

That's why sales of this book will raise funds for Walsall Healthcare NHS Trust's Well Wishers charity to support the Critical Care Rehabilitation Team, which is helping Covid patients and others on their road to recovery.

DT

PROLOGUE:

The Year, 1BC (Before Covid)

The day the virus came, I was out.

Fortunately, my neighbour Doris was at home, so the courier gave it to her, and she passed it on to her family and friends; she gave it to her workmates, the local corner shop, the hairdressers, the Ring and Ride driver, his three passengers, the dentist, the dental receptionist and who knows how many thousands of others. But, to my eternal shame and guilt, she did not give it to me – the one it was intended for.

Perhaps I should explain.

I am convinced, you see, from all I've read since, that the Covid Lockdown was my fault. I realise that's quite a big claim – although to be fair I have made bigger ones on my house insurance - but I believe it to be the truth, the whole truth and something like the truth. It's a long story. And it's quite a journey.

So strap yourselves in, and I'll take it from the top.

First of all, it's pretty much accepted by top scientists that the virus came from China. When I say 'top scientists', you have to bear in mind that I was getting all my information first-hand from the horse's stable, after speaking with Sharon Daniels (one of the women I met at Bingo, in the days when you could meet women at Bingo) and Sharon's daughter Juniper has a Bachelor of Arts degree in Physics, and a Diploma in Marketing.

So I'm afraid there's no disputing the hard, cold facts. A respected academic, with an IQ in excess of a hundred, has confirmed it. So how does that connect to me?

Well, it just so happens that just six weeks before the pandango hit Britain, I ordered a battery-powered kitchen scrubber off Facebook. I was impressed by the video of the rotating plastic brush head, and I thought it would really help speed Doris up when she cleaned for me (she does seem to have been slowing down a bit lately). So, as a special surprise for her, I borrowed Doris's credit card and placed the order. What I now know, but didn't at the time, was that it would take another six weeks to arrive, and that it was coming from China.

Clearly, the virus was attached to the parcel, and that's how it entered the UK undetected. The timing is too much of a coincidence. Yes, I know that to the lawyers amongst you, the evidence may only seem circumcisional - but hear me out.

Less than three days after receiving the parcel, Doris came down with a runny nose and started to feel a bit tired. Remember, this is Doris we're talking about. Doris has never had a day off work in her life – not even the time she was run over – but later that week she overslept and rang me to ask if she could be excused from doing my washing. I'm not one to hold a grudge, so I grudgingly agreed – but it wasn't like her, and I began to wonder if there was more to this than just a random bout of laziness.

Then I heard that the bloke in the corner shop was self-insulating, on account of something he'd heard on the news about a new virus - something that everyone except Donald Trump was scared to say came from China.

Now, I have a lot of time for the Chinese. Like me, they're hard-working, and also like me, they eat Chinese food. And they've also invented some great things throughout history, such as fireworks, great walls and rotating kitchen scrubbers. But, sadly, a small percentage of their modest 1.5 billion population apparently also occasionally shares Ozzie Osbourne's habit of casually chewing on bats.

The problem is that bats, if not cooked properly (puncture lid, three minutes in the microwave, stir and then another two minutes) can play havoc with the digestive system, or worse still, cause a global health crisis and cripple the world's economy for decades. And it seems that on this occasion that's what may have happened.

You may be wondering why I'm convinced that it was my parcel from China that caused the problem, and not somebody else's. After all, I couldn't have been the only one importing goods from Asia that week – in fact, I hear that the bloke running Amazon also had quite a busy month, as his personal fortune increased from $150 billion to just over $180 billion. That, surely, must have affected his Universal Credit payments, if they have those in America.

Well, anyway - the reason I can pinpoint the virus as being on my parcel with such certainty is quite simple.

The chances of two separate viruses being on two separate parcels from China is a little too far-fetched for any rational person to believe, so we're left with the damning evidence of Doris's runny nose and tiredness happening within hours of answering the doorbell to my courier.

Furthermore, Doris has since told me that she didn't touch

any other parcel that week, except my normal food parcel from the food bank (I find it's cheaper than Sainsbury's) and that's something I've had many times before with no issues.

So, those are the facts, laid bare before you. I wish they weren't the facts, of course. I wish I could turn back the clocks. In fact I did, in October, and I ended up with an extra hour in bed, which is always nice. But it's no use you pointing the finger at me, or even two fingers, because it's easy to be wise with eyesight, and I've lost track of the number of times I've blamed myself. I think it was twice.

If only I'd not looked at Facebook that day and seen that battery-powered scrubber, and if only Doris had made a better job of hiding her credit card, then everything might have been different.

But it's too late for the blame game – the bat is out of the bag - and now I fear we've all got to learn to live with the consequences.

And so, dear readers, to the point of this book.

Yes, there is one.

Because I know that Lockdown has been very tough for many folk, me included. But, gradually, I learnt to adapt – to find new strategies to cope. No, I didn't always get things right. In fact, in some ways, I never got things right. But my spirit stayed strong. And most importantly of all, I refused to give up. Ever. Not even just after I may have hinted to that I had actually given up, by screaming "Fuck it, I give up" at the top of my voice, in front of dozens of witnesses at the Co-op.

And so I thought that by sharing my trials, tribulations and triumphs with you all, it may just bring some small crumbs of comfort to those in dark places, such as underneath my stairs. Doris still hasn't changed the bulb.

That's why you'll find the pages that follow are crammed with life-changing tips on how I got through lockdown. Hopefully, they will now also help you to get through not just this crisis, but any crisis.

These are my Covid Chronicles – The Secret Diary of a Lazy Cow in Lockdown.

I hope it helps.

COVID CHRONICLES

LOCKDOWN BEGINS
23rd March, 2020

Last week, on the 16th March, a politician bloke I'd never heard of by the name of Matt Hancock told the House of Commons that "all unnecessary social contact should cease."

At the time, this wasn't a big deal to me. After all, I've often thought all unnecessary social contact should cease. In fact, I'd already ceased it myself many years earlier.

But today, it all suddenly became very real.

I've switched on the telly news, and with all the gravitarse of a wartime Churchill, Boris Johnson, the newly-erected Prime Minister, has just confirmed that people now 'must' stay at home, unless, in extreme circumstances, they don't want to.

This, I sense, is very serious.

Businesses have been told to shut. You now can't visit a dentist, or a Job Centre. And weddings have been banned.

But it's not all good news.

Pubs are also being forced to close. So are Bingo Halls and Casinos. Millions of folk are being told that they are to receive money just for staying at home – something I've been advocating for years, but never thought any Tory politician would ever agree to.

Even teachers (who are not normally work-shy) are trying

to get used to the totally alien idea of having a really long extended summer holiday on full pay.

Lockdown had begun. And for the very first time since I ordered the kitchen-scrubber, I started to feel a deep sense of guilt – but also a deep sense of grievance. After all, if working folk were now going to be paid just for staying at home, where did that leave me? Surely I then would need a decent increase in Universal Credit just to maintain my differential?

But this is a national crisis, and no time to be selfish. After all, there's no such thing as a free lunch, unless you go to a Food Bank, so one day in the future all this hand-out money will have to be paid back, with interest. When that day comes, it's the tax-payers that will be hit hardest. And I feel for them.

Anyway, today, in anticipation of all that is to come, I told Doris to buy me a diary. I intend to record my innermost thoughts at this difficult time and, one day, perhaps I will share them with you.

24th March

Doris did get me the diary, and I am recording and sharing my innermost thoughts at this difficult time, so you can ignore the previous sentence from yesterday.

Tomorrow I will start on my diary in earnest. I will be nothing less than a latter-day Samuel Pepys.

Can't be arsed to write any more today, though.

Celebrity Tipping Point is on.

25th March

I've been watching the telly news again, to get abreast of all the public information messages.

Apparently, the key to not getting this virus is to wash your hands. That's easy enough. The hard bit is turning off the tap afterwards, because then it might be contaminated. If you turn it off by hand (which I find easier than using my feet) you could pick up a germ from it, so you then need to wash your hands again.

This, of course, involves turning the tap back on again, and then off again, which in turn might involve getting another germ from it. So then you need to wash your hands again.

As I found out to my cost, this can go on all day. Good job I'm not on a water meter. It took me a while to work out how to deal with this.

In the end I got Doris to turn the taps on and off, and then made her go home to wash her hands, and then come back and swill off my taps. You can't be too careful.

31st March

It's the end of week one, and this is already more serious than I first thought. I'm getting very low on toilet rolls. I've only got seventeen multipacks left. That's down to all these idiots stockpiling.

Next time, I'll tell Doris to empty the shop of all they've got, so the stockpilers can't have any.

It'll serve them right.

1st April

A bloke on TV just said it's April Fool's Day, but I'm not sure whether or not to believe him.

2nd April

Restrictions are tightening now.

Doris is getting a bit worried about being spotted popping round to my house every day – especially with that nosy Nazi curtain-twitching cow Brenda over the road.

She's the sort that would report her own grandchildren and have them locked up. In fact, she has. Though to be fair, they did actually need locking up. Remind me one day to tell you what the little bastards did with the tortoise and some Gaffa tape.

So anyway, Doris and I have hatched a plan. I watched a film last week called 'The Great Escape.' I'd never heard of it before, even though Doris reckons it's occasionally put on at Christmas, but it gave me an idea.

Doris is going to try and persuade her husband, Jack, to excavate a tunnel between my house and theirs, so she can still come round and do my ironing unseen by prying neighbours. Apparently there's a separating wall that isn't load-bearing, whatever that means, which would let her get from under her stairs into my pantry.

Doris is going to hide the rubble up her trousers, and spread it around the garden while pretending to exercise, so nobody will ever know. I did offer to help do that, but Doris pointed out that none of the neighbours would ever

10

believe I was exercising, so I decided to leave it all to her.

Jack might take a bit of persuading – he can be a stubborn bugger sometimes – but hopefully Doris will convince him that it's a very sensible and practical idea.

She'll be back to tell me how she got on later, under the cover of darkness.

2nd April, 9.30pm

Apparently, Jack said no.

3rd April

I told Doris to have another go at Jack.

I reckon he didn't take the plan seriously because it was the day after April Fool's Day. But Doris was reluctant. Apparently he didn't just say no. He said lots of other words as well. In fact, I think I might have heard some of them through the adjoining wall.

Jack's got a bit of a nasty temper on him sometimes. But to be fair, he can also be as good as gold. If you're ever in trouble or need anything, you can always rely on Jack to lend you his wife.

7th April

I've had a few days off from writing the diary.

The ball-point ran out and I had to wait for Doris to get me another off the internet. She got a pack of two, so I should be all right for a bit.

I saw the Queen on telly a couple of days ago. She said "We'll meet again." I can't remember meeting her the first time, to be honest, but she's the Queen so she must be right. And then yesterday they said that Boris Johnson had gone into hospital with the virus.

I wish I'd never ordered the bloody kitchen scrubber.

Turns out it was shite anyway. The video shows it tearing through dirt and grime like a power drill. But Doris says that the moment you touch anything with it, it just stops. Then it takes another two days to charge it up. Not really worth twenty-four quid to be honest, and certainly not worth a worldwide financial crash. I told Doris to try and get her money back.

10th April

Today should have been the first night of my new show 'Revolution' – the start of my annual Midlands tour.

Had this wretched virus not kicked off I would have been standing on the stage at Dudley Town Hall now, with over a thousand folk, all having a loff.

We booked all the theatres two years ago to make sure we got prime slots – all Saturday nights – and it was pretty much all sold-out. But now the whole lot has had to be cancelled and re-scheduled for next spring.

It's a total bitch, but I suppose if I follow my own logic and the virus turns out to be all my fault, then I shouldn't really complain. But I will anyway.

A lot of other people have re-scheduled their shows for the autumn this year. I think they might be being optimistic. I've got a horrible feeling that this mess isn't going to be sorted that quickly.

Some folks are even saying that the Christmas pantos might be affected. And all because of my Amazon parcel and its rubbish kitchen scrubber. We'll see.

Looking on the bright side, there are some benefits to the tour being cancelled. For a start, I don't have to get out of bed till early evening. And I also now don't have to learn the script.

Learning words gets a lot harder as you get older.

I've started using a clipboard on stage, because for some reason a lot of people think that clipboards can make you look quite important and intelligent, whereas in reality people with clipboards are usually boring twats that are best avoided.

Anyway, I don't really care if people do think I'm a bit boring – they'd probably think I was a lot more boring if I just stood on stage and didn't speak because I couldn't remember my words.

Having a clipboard is just a safety net - it means I will definitely remember what to say. Though now I do find I sometimes forget other things, such as where I've left my clipboard.

To play safe, the next time I'm on tour I'm going to make sure that the very first thing I write on the top of the clipboard is where I've left it.

10th May

The Government have changed the public message from '**Stay at Home**' to '**Stay Alert**'.

I prefer to stay at home. I've never been very alert. It's just not in my nature. They also said that folk can now exercise more than once a day. Luckily there was no mention of this being compulsory.

11th May

Fuck all happened today.

12th May

There are rumours that this lockdown may last longer than three weeks.

13th July

The rumours were true.

14th July

According to Doris, we're now into the third month of this three-week lockdown. No wonder I thought time was passing slowly.

These days I tend to get all my information from Doris. I no longer trust any other source of news. Unlike the BBC, I know Doris wouldn't lie to me. She's been working for me for too long.

Doris, of course, gets all her information from Jack, who's a self-employed plumber and decorator, so he gets all his information first-hand, from folks at the pub. And the word on the streets is that it's all a conspiracy, apparently, to control us. The State wants us all to just stay at home and live off benefits.

It's a disgrace. Yes, of course I'll do my bit, as always, but Doris needs to work.

15th July

The Job Centres have reopened. Bastards.

They're advocating social distancing, so I'm keeping a couple of miles away. I might get Doris to pop in at some point though and ask if there do some sort of Job Centre version of furloughing. In other words, they find me a job, which I obviously can't do because of lockdown, and then pay me 80% of the salary to stay at home.

I reckon I'd be quite good at that sort of job. But Doris reckons I'd probably be worse off than I am on Universal Credit, unless they furlough me on the wage of a skilled worker, such as an airline pilot, dentist, or a head teacher or something.

Well, the way I see it, there's no reason why it shouldn't be a highly-skilled job, as I wouldn't be doing it anyway. If I'm being paid to stay at home all day I might as well be furloughed as a brain surgeon – nobody would ever know.

She said she'd ask, anyway.

16th July

Doris said the man at the Job Centre wasn't too helpful.

He called security.

17th July

Doris suggested I try a spot of gardening.

She said it'd be good for my mental health, so I've made a start by asking Jack to concrete over my window box. It's too high maintenance.

I've also come up with a gardening work rota. On the second and fourth weeks of the month, Doris can cut my lawn. And on the first and third weeks, I'll just give it time to grow. I'm also cultivating a nettle garden.

18th July

I've decided to ask Doris to grow my own tomatoes.

They're hard work, apparently. And for people on a water meter, such as Doris, they usually average out at about seventeen quid per tomato, which is even more than Asda charge.

But it'll be good for her mental health, so money's not everything. Especially if it's not my money.

And, of course, if the tomatoes come out all right, I'll let Doris have some. That's only fair, as she'll be using her own greenhouse.

Besides, I don't actually like tomatoes.

21st July

Lockdown is playing havoc with my hair.

Well, I say hair – it's about one inch of hair and eighteen inches of roots. I look like a fucking punk badger.

I've asked Doris to pop round and remove all the mirrors.

But there may be a light at the end of the funnel. Doris has ordered one of them electric trimmer things from the internet. It's not from China, so hopefully it'll take less than a year to arrive, and then she can do my hair properly.

23rd July

Doris's gadget arrived today.

Not as advertised. It's a strimmer, not a trimmer. Designed mainly for hedges. But I told her she can still come round later and have a go at my hair. It can't get any worse.

24th July

It got worse.

25th July

I couldn't face writing any more yesterday.

I was too traumatised after the haircut. I now look like a badger that's had a collision with a tractor. Doris is still sweeping up the hair from the kitchen floor, and she's ordered a skip. But at least her new gadget worked quite well on the hedges.

I've asked her to trim my bush next time she comes round, but she wasn't enthusiastic. She's hard work sometimes. But trimming a bush is less painful than waxing.

15th August

Another big Government announcement.

'Close-contact' beauty services were able to resume work from today. Good for them. I bet they've really missed my business.

They also announced that wedding receptions with up to thirty guests are now permitted. A lot of folk are moaning about that, saying that it'll ruin their big day, but when I nearly got married I didn't have any guests at all. Just two witnesses, both provided by the police.

Luckily the main culprit didn't turn up. In fact he's not been seen since.

I think we both had a lucky escape.

19th August

No Doris today.

She's having to do a double shift at work, cleaning the supermarket, because her friend is off sick. Not Corona apparently, though it'll probably go down as that if she dies. Hopefully that's unlikely though, as she's only got frostbite from cleaning out one of the fridges.

And to make things worse, Doris then sprained her ankle when she slipped on a bag of frozen peas. The nurse said it wasn't broken, just swollen, and told her to put a bag of frozen peas on it.

She says she might be able to get here about six.

6.03pm

Still no Doris.

She rang me to say her ankle's getting worse, and she's having to do quadruple shifts now because three more staff have gone down with frostbite, so could I possibly cook my own tea tonight. It's a bit much to be honest. Doris needs to be more careful where she's treading.

But anyway, I've already done all the spade-work now – I've phoned the pizza bloke. He says they have to be careful about social distancing, but he's offered to chuck a ten-inch Hawaiian over the hedge in about 15 minutes.

I'll report back. ˎ

8pm

Just collected the pizza box from the garden.

There's fuck all in it. The pizza bloke's going to get a rocket.

I'll report back.

8.40pm

Mystery solved.

Pizza bloke was adamant that there was an Hawaiian in there, so I double–checked. Well, perhaps there was when it left his hand, but it must have parted company with the cardboard box when he chucked it, because I eventually found it in the rhododendron bush.

If he thinks they're going to get paid for this he's mistaken. I ordered a pizza, not a fucking Frisbee.

A new one is on its way.

9.10pm

The second pizza was okay.

In fact, the first wasn't too bad either. Better than I was expecting, given the visual state of it. It looked like it had been dragged through a hedge backwards, mainly because it had.

Tasted okay, but still not as nice as Doris's home cooking.

Hope her ankle mends soon. If not, she'll have to cook on crutches.

20th August

Doris is still bed-ridden.

I wouldn't mind if she had some sort of syndrome, but this is beginning to look like pure laziness. It's far easier to fake physical ailments - I should know.

21st August

Loneliness can be a strange thing.

I never thought I'd do this, but I've made friends with a fly. Usually I just try and belt the little bastards with a newspaper, but this one's been with me for two days now (he was a bit too quick for me) and I think we've started to form a bond.

He sits listening to me, which is more than most humans do. I'm sure that, if he could, he'd read my book. I even started wondering if I could somehow hear his side of the story.

It can't be much fun being a fly. Nobody really wants you around. Anyway, I think there's a definite mutual respect there now, and I'll be sad to see him go.

Having said that, if he lands on my food again it'll tip me over the edge and I'll put out a contract out on him. I'd have to ask Doris to come round with some fly spray. I've tended not to use the stuff myself, not since the time I couldn't find my glasses and I accidentally blasted a fly with some Asda firm-hold hair lacquer.

The force of the spray blew him sideways, he flew over a candle, exploded and set fire to the curtains. It's been newspapers for me ever since. For killing flies, I mean - not for covering up the windows.

Doris doesn't like having to wipe the mess off the glass, but as I explained to her, it's better than her having to trek into town to order me some new curtains every week. Not to mention buying new cans of hair spray.

22nd August

No sign of the fly today.

23rd August

The fly is back. We're just going to have a quiet night in.

24th August

Do flies sleep?

This one doesn't seem to. But surely they must. I'll get Doris to look it up for me on the internet.

25th August

Doris went on the internet and found some fascinating facts about flies.

Apparently flies do sleep, usually at night. If they don't, it can affect their ability to concentrate – a bit like me. And baby flies apparently need more sleep.

Sharks, however, according to Doris, don't sleep. So I'm glad I don't currently have a shark on my ceiling. It'd be waiting for me to doze off and then attack. And as far as I know, Asda don't do shark spray.

Anyway, I'm glad that flies sleep. I thought they would.

Flying when you're tired must be dangerous, even for experienced flyers, like flies. I know that they don't have passengers, so it's just their own risk, but even so.

Actually, I think I've been in lockdown too long.

31st August

I've just told Doris to limp outside on my behalf and clap for the NHS.

I couldn't be arsed. I've had my issues with them in the past. They made me wait over a year to see a consultant, and in the end he told me there was nothing wrong with me. That's not what you want to hear from a doctor.

Anyway, I don't remember the NHS staff ever standing outside and clapping me, and I'm a paying customer. And it's getting harder during lockdown to make any sort of appointment. The quickest way to see a doctor these days is to become a nurse.

I think the training period is sixteen weeks.

32nd August

Doris is finally....hang on a bit.

I'm not even sure there is a 32nd of August. That's the last time I let Doris buy cheap diaries from Bilston market. Just checked the small print. Made in fucking China. That figures.

1st September

Doris is finally back on duty, albeit still with a limp.

But she says that from now on we need to keep two metres apart. How she's going to manage that while cutting my toenails tonight I don't really know, but that's her problem. And to be fair she is a marvel – she'll find a way round the rules somehow, even if it means catching the virus.

26th November

Just checked, and my last diary entry was 1st September, so if you've been wondering where I've been for the last three months, sorry about that. I'm back now.

Doris did a bit of a tidy up when she came back on duty, and I haven't been able to find the fucking diary for nearly a quarter of a year.

I've now just finally come across it, underneath the tea towel. I'd looked everywhere. Well, except under the tea towel, obviously. Twelve weeks of my life, lost forever. That's a whole season. And it's no good me asking me to try and remember what's been happening all that time. Very little probably. But that's not the point.

That woman's in for a bollocking.

27th November

Doris came in to clean today, so I tackled her about the missing diary.

She said I should have just asked her about it ages ago, because she knew all along that it was underneath the tea towel. She said that's where I'd left it, and she didn't want to move it somewhere else in case I then couldn't find it.

That woman's got an answer for everything.

As if I'd leave a diary under a tea towel. As if I'd even touch a tea towel. The only reason I touched one recently was because I couldn't find my tissues. I was livid.

Anyway, we're back on track now. Back in Samuel Pepys mode. From now on, I'll try and do an entry every few days. And from now on, I'll also keep the diary on top of the tea towel. That way I'll know exactly where it is.

28th November

Minor scare just. Doris had moved the tea towel to wash it. Luckily, the diary was still there, on top of the missing tea towel.

Panic over, but she's becoming a liability. She just can't stop meddling with things. I feel like my house just isn't my own any more.

29th November

I just read that there's now an outbreak of 'bird flu' at a turkey farm in North Yorkshire.

It's not going well, this year, is it?

Perhaps the turkey farmer took delivery of a parcel from Amazon. I just hope there's not an outbreak of 'pigs in blankets flu' at the Asda.

Merry Christmas.

30th November

Apparently, according to Doris, I'm now allowed to see my family at Christmas.

I don't want to.

For a start off, I'm not 100% sure who some of them are, and also it always ends in tantrums. The kids are at an age now where they prefer to be left alone, which is quite lucky, as one of them is in solitary confinement.

Our Trojan has always had a quick temper on her, and to

be fair she can sometimes be a bit mouthy, unlike her sister, Tangerine, who's a lot mouthy. But Tange's bark is worse than her bite, whereas Trojan's bite is very painful.

Sometimes Trojan speaks before she thinks. Other times she attacks people physically before she thinks, and that's probably what's landed her in trouble more than once. Eight times actually, which is more than once.

Attacking the police is not a great career move usually, though to be fair she hasn't had to pay for a single meal since, and she now lives rent-free with access to a well-equipped gym, and they've got Sky telly and a ping pong table, so it's not all bad news.

2nd December

Sorry I've been away from the diary for a while. I've been trying to catch up on the latest regulations – there's been a lot going on lately.

As I understand it from my insider source (Doris, via Jack) we've just had a second lockdown (I didn't notice) and then today on December 2nd we came out of the second lockdown straight into Tier 3.

This is where it gets complicated.

It turns out that Tier 3 is another name for lockdown, so they could have called it Lockdown 3 instead, except they can't because it doesn't apply everywhere - just to places where people live, except London, which is a special case because that's where politicians live.

Anyway, the reason we need a third lockdown is because

the second lockdown didn't work, so we need to try it again but change its name, which should mean that it works this time. And if it doesn't work again this time, we'll give it one last go, before finally re-branding it and giving it another last go a few more times.

By this time it should be spring, and then the amount of cases will go down dramatically, proving what a success all the previous lockdowns were.

At this point, according to Doris (I think she gets a lot of her information from Jack, who reads a lot at the pub) the entire wealth of the world will soon be owned by just four blokes – the bloke who owns Apple, the bloke who owns Facebook, the bloke who owns China, and the bloke who owns Amazon.

Nobody else will have any money whatsoever.

And that's a problem for the bloke who owns Amazon.

Doris says that Amazon will then employ everybody in the world (except China), and their job will be to buy things from Amazon, which will then come from China a year later, having been advertised on Facebook.

My worry is, there might be another virus attached to one of the parcels, and the whole lot could kick off again. I'm not sure I could cope with this a second time. I've already coped with it three times.

3rd December

Started my second stint in Tier 3 today.

It didn't feel a great deal different to normal, to be honest.

Except the gyms are shut. That's what will affect me the most, but only in a positive way.

Doris used to help clean some of the gyms. Now she can spend more time cleaning here.

5th December

There's a lot of politics going on in Britain.

I don't follow it all, but it seems the Brexit negotiation deadline is nearing an end, so it'll need to be extended again to give us a new deadline, which can obviously be extended again when we reach that one. This will go on until everyone who voted for Brexit has died, and then we can finally forget about it for good. As I understand it (and I probably don't) there are currently three major stumbling blocks to signing a deal.

First, the EU want all our fish, but in a last-minute heroic gesture they're willing to compromise and only have 82% of our fish. Personally, I think the fish should get a vote, but that's logistically tricky. I'm sure any self-respecting cod would like to end up in a proper British fish and chip shop rather than some foreign one.

Secondly, the EU want a level playing field. That basically means that they can do what they want, but we can't do anything unless they agree.

And finally, in the event of a dispute between us and them, they want to be the ones who decide who's right.

It seems to me that the EU are being very fair, and our bloke's being a bit stubborn and selfish, because he's only thinking about Britain's interests. But I don't really claim to know all the details.

A free trade deal is important, apparently, however much it costs. Let's imagine it in simple terms that we can all understand.

Let's say I went into a foreign shop, and wanted to buy a Mars Bar. The foreign shop bloke might say "You can have the Mars Bar for free, because it's a free Mars Bar." I'd say "Thanks very much." And the shop bloke would say, "But there is a fee to enter the shop." And I'd say, "How much?" And he'd say, "£39 billion quid a year. And while you're here, give me all your fish."

Now, to my mind that's an expensive Mars Bar, but the export experts say it isn't, and they know best.

6th December

Doris says that everybody who goes outside or into shops has to wear a mask now.

I just wish that sort of regulation had been in place a few years back when my daughters got done for shoplifting. A decent lawyer would have made mince-meat of all the CCTV evidence.

They used to say you couldn't go into a bank or a petrol station if you were wearing a mask. Now they say you can't go into bank or petrol station unless you *are* wearing a mask. It's sending out a bit of a mixed message, and thieves must be having a field day, whatever that means. I've never been sure what's so good about having a day in a field.

7th December

I got Doris to look up the phrase 'Having A Field Day' on her computer.

According to Wankepedia, it comes from when they used to have wars in muddy fields in the 1800s. A good day in the field was when you'd killed lots of the enemy. Hence the military title Field Marshal.

This lockdown is becoming a bit like a war, to be honest. A war with an invisible enemy. Trouble is, nobody knows who the real enemy is any more. Is it the virus? Is it the Government? Is it the bloke from Amazon?

There's hundreds of conspiracy theories about. I've been reading about them and it's made my head spin.

Some folks reckon that the virus is totally made up and nobody has really got it. Others, mainly the ones who've got it, reckon they're wrong.

Some newspapers say the hospitals are rammed, others say they're half-empty.

Some say the nurses and doctors are at breaking point, others say they spend all day making TikTok videos and playing poker – a bit like the Fire Brigade.

Some experts say you can have no symptoms whatsoever, but still pass the Covid virus on.

Other experts say that asymptomatic people don't tend to pass it on. And a third lot say the reason you don't tend to pass it on if you have no symptoms is because you haven't actually got it.

And you can see their point.

One bloke I read about on Faceache had sent for a test, popped it straight back in the post without doing it, and it came back positive.

Another bloke dipped the swab stick into a bottle of Coca Cola, and that came back positive as well. So it's hard to know who to believe.

Talking of Coca Cola, I've noticed lately that they've now stopped calling the virus 'Corona' (which coincidentally used to be a brand of fizzy pop in the Black Country) and re-branded it Covid. Don't know why.

It might be to do with too many people taking the piss out of the Corona name in songs. Covid sounds a lot more serious.

It seems that these days even viruses can have marketing agencies working for them.

Anyway, back to the debate. Personally, I think we need to trust the experts. But that's hard, because the experts don't trust the experts, so why should we? But let's be honest, when have you ever known an expert be wrong?

Well, pretty much every fucking time.

In economics, politics, and health. But they're still experts, and they still get paid loads to be experts. And the TV folk still invite them back on the news to be experts again.

Of course, on social media, everybody's an expert. And this is my book, so that makes me an expert.

What we really need in the modern world is to get back to the idea of experts having some sort of expertise.

But that's not going to happen, in my expert view.

8th December

It's probably a good job my daughters are still detained at Her Majesty's pleasure.

For a start off, two fewer mouths to feed. But also, I'm not sure how they'd handle the shops all being shut. It'd play havoc with their takings.

I wonder if the Chancellor of the Exchequebook has ever thought about whether shoplifters should be furloughed on 80% of their usual income? I doubt it. Once again a hard-hit minority would slip through the cracks.

I also believe young offenders generally should get some sort of financial compensation when they're taken off the streets. After all, it saves money on policing, so that cash should be reinvested in their future.

I know that our Trojan has been working on some sort of online training course for young shoplifters, so perhaps that could be funded centrally by the Government. After all, if she makes enough from that, she can stand on her own two feet and wouldn't have to steal any longer, so it's a win-win.

If you can't do it, teach it.

9th December

Just watched yet another Government announcement.

These daily briefings now seem to be happening every 24 hours. The latest one left me a bit baffled. I tried to write it down, but Doris wasn't around to pass me a pen.

Here's how Doris explained it to me afterwards:

dreary, slightly blurred things that have been made to look like they were shot on iPhones by grinning building society clerks working from home with a cat, while we all know they were made by ad agencies charging a fortune.

And I'm sorry, but if I have to listen to just one more street-cred poet saying "We're all in this togevver" while he's delivering a pizza, I'll lob a house brick at the telly. It's pretentious shite. Shite with extra cheese.

Then there's the Black Friday adverts. Christ. Yet another dreadful import from America.

"Well," you could argue, "at least it's only for one day."

Is it bollocks.

Have you noticed over the past couple of years how the Black Friday sale has gradually morphed into the Black Friday weekend, Black Friday mega-week, Black Friday month, Black Friday re-booted, Black Friday leap year, Black Friday decade, and Black Friday lifetime?

Then, just as you think they've squeezed all they can from what is basically a shit sale, up pops the new kid on the block - Cyber fucking Monday, which then lasts another six months to take us neatly into Christmas.

Then of course we have the Christmas adverts themselves. Jesus Christ. No actually, he doesn't come into it.

It's now just become a race (and I use the word advisedly) to see which organisation can go the extra mile to look the most virtuous and politically correct.

For a start, it seems that you can't even eat an oven chip or order a sofa these days unless your family ticks all the PC boxes at once. As an absolute minimum standard you have to be married to, or co-habiting with, somebody who's a different colour from you, and if you can't manage that you have to be gay or disabled – ideally all three.

And no – being ginger doesn't seem to count.

Personally, I like a bit of diversity, so it's a shame that we don't really get any on TV ads any longer.

Why? Because every single family on television now has to have exactly the same tick-box ingredients, one of each.

I happen to be white (an accident of birth) but I can only guess that it might be just as annoying for black people to know that only one of them is allowed per ideal advert family.

How did we get here?

Well, as usual, political correctness starts off as a great idea - to try and represent everybody, including minorities. But then, driven by slightly nutty zealous types whose job title now demands diversity at all costs, it then becomes an exaggerated obsession, until finally, by disproportionately trying to represent absolutely everybody, in every single advert, every single time, they usually end up representing nobody, except possibly a circus act.

And then, of course, reluctantly squeezed in between the adverts, you get the occasional programme. But let's face it, there's only so many old episodes of Tipping Point you can watch before you reach your own tipping point and go into a coma.

Anyway. It'll be Christmas soon.

Perhaps there'll be a film on. Hopefully one with a proper bit of talent-led diversity. Such as that Morgan Freeman bloke. Or Idris Elba. Or Will Smith. Or Sidney Poitier. Or Denzel Washington. Or Lenny…

No, perhaps not Lenny Henry. After all, he's from Dudley.

11th December

I've been trying to keep up with the American elections.

It's a bit confusing. As I understand it, a bloke called Joe Biden won when they found loads of lost ballot papers in a suitcase, so they made everybody wait outside for a few hours while an impartial team of Joe Biden supporters counted them, and found that they were all for him.

Also, it seems, in America, dead people are still allowed to vote. That's a good rule I reckon.

I usually find it too hard to vote, just because I'm a bit tired. So if a dead person is willing to make the effort to get out and vote, then good luck to them – they deserve to be part of the process. Dead people are also easier to govern – fewer protests – though to be fair they don't pay any taxes, so they shouldn't expect too much.

I don't know what's going to happen next.

Donald Trump is taking it all to the Supreme Court, where apparently the judges don't take as many bribes. Bigger ones, yes, but not as many.

I think it'll all end up in a bit of a row, or worse – a lot of a row.

16th December

There's been another Government review of the whole Tier thing today.

I've been moved out of Tier 3 into Tier 12 – it's a bit rough round here to be honest. I'm not surprised.

It's only a temporary measure, apparently, just until I die.

That does mean I'm technically no longer allowed to see Doris, so we're revisiting plans to knock the wall through from her house to mine. Jack's not going to be too pleased about it, but Doris has borrowed a lump-hammer, and we're hoping to get it done while he's asleep.

Jack's a heavy sleeper. I know that for a fact, from when we went to the caravan with him. He could sleep through a violent burglary. In fact, he did.

On the first night there I woke up to see the caravan door wide open, and some shadowy figure rifling through my purse in the night, so I crept up behind and twatted them with a saucepan. It sounded like a gigantic dinner gong going off. Doris woke up with a start and instantly weed the bed. But Jack slept through the whole thing. So did Trojan, actually, who I later discovered was the one who was going through my purse.

Serves her right. If she wants money all she has to do is ask. I'd have said no, of course, but it's the principle that counts.

So anyway, Operation Great Escape is set for tonight.

It's all meticulously planned. Doris is going to slip Jack a couple of extra glasses of whiskey to anaesthetise him.

Then, hopefully around midnight, she'll disappear into the cupboard under her stairs, and then emerge heroically through the rubble into my pantry.

It's a bit like the Channel Tunnel, except my tunnel won't let any foreigners in. Not even Jack, who's technically foreign, as he's a Brummie.

I've actually got nothing against Jack using the tunnel, as it happens, but Doris is hoping that she can keep it a secret from him, as he never looks in the cupboard under the stairs.

It's where she keeps the hoover, and Jack's old-fashioned like that.

17th December

It's all kicked off next-door.

Apparently, on the very first swing of the lump-hammer, Doris hit a mains water pipe. It was bad. Jack eventually woke up when he felt his feet getting wet upstairs.

I felt a bit sorry for Doris. The water almost immediately tripped all the electrics, so Doris was groping in the dark for twenty minutes trying to find her phone, using just the torch on her phone, until she finally realised that the phone was already in her hand, pretending to be a torch. Then, just as she got through to the emergency plumber, the battery on her phone died.

She managed to find Jack's phone when she trod on it, and tried again.

The emergency plumber said he couldn't come straight

away, but he'd put a quote in the post, and as an expert tip he recommended that she switched the water off at the stop-cock.

So poor Doris was left for hours, on her own in the pitch black, trying to find the stop-cock, without really knowing what a stop-cock was. She told me later that she thought it was a form of contraceptive.

Eventually she had to casually ask Jack where it was, when he waded into the hall looking damp and bewildered in a dressing gown. He said that the stop-cock was under the stairs.

That wasn't great news. Apparently, it was the stop-cock that Doris had hit with the lump-hammer, so there was now no way to turn off her water without disconnecting the whole street.

She then phoned the water people, and an answering machine said her call was very important to them, but due to Covid they couldn't answer the phone, ever.

Doris's lounge was now beginning to resemble a scene from Titanic. Doris was calling for Jack a lot, just like in the film, and her furniture was floating sideways. The goldfish had now made its way from the bowl to the kitchen sink, which it seemed to favour. More leg room, I suppose. Not that fish have legs.

In the end, Doris had the good sense to open the front door to get the water levels down a bit. My front lawn's still a quagmire, so hopefully she'll put that right one day. I won't trouble her with it yet, though, I think she's got a lot on at the moment.

It's a shame. The tunnel was essentially a very good idea, until Doris mishandled it. In retrospect I should have been there to direct proceedings, but I can't do everything.

Eventually, in fact at four o'clock the next afternoon, an emergency plumber arrived after finishing an emergency game of golf. He examined the scene, and concluded that the stop-cock had suffered a blunt force trauma, possibly from a lump-hammer or similar, probably wielded by a right-handed female attacker, around five feet seven tall with brown hair. Time of death, around midnight.

He was good. But not cheap. He fixed the leak and then made Doris hand over more cash than a Mexican drugs baron.

Jack went ballistic. Partly because he's a plumber, and he didn't get the job. And he would have gone even more ballistic had he known the full story.

Doris is denying all knowledge of how it happened, and she's hidden the lump-hammer behind the hoover, where Jack will never find it. But I fear that one day, he will discover the truth.

Possibly when he reads this book.

18th December

Doris is desperately trying to tidy up the almighty mess at her house before Christmas.

I decided to help her all I could, by telling her not to bother coming round to do my washing and hoovering today, so she can concentrate on her own mess.

She was very grateful, but that's what friends are for.

Everything she owns is now on her front lawn, drying out. It's not easy, because it's raining. I even said she could borrow some of my own lawn space if she needed it – as long as it was all shifted by Christmas Day.

19th December

Doris reckons a vaccine is on its way.

Some people are very wary of vaccines, especially ones knocked together in ten minutes with a kids' chemistry set and a Harry Potter spell book. Usually, human vaccines take decades to produce and to test. And even then, things can go a bit wrong, like people start growing antlers or something.

I'm not sure how I feel about having the vaccine, to be honest. Apparently it's only a tiny prick, and I've seen plenty of those before.

But you do have to wonder how rigorously and honestly they'll be testing it, when the reward for passing the test is probably a Nobel Prize, plus about 15 billion quid in untraceable cash. That sort of money pays for quite a few scientific opinions.

Not that I'm suggesting that anybody in big business or politics is corrupt. That's never happened, ever. But I think that even I'd be tempted to cut a few corners if I was them:

"Yeah, okay – so we didn't know that it'd make you grow antlers, but at least you haven't had Covid yet."

Thankfully, it seems it won't be compulsory to have the jab. But if you don't have it, you can never go on a bus again, or a train, or a plane, or in a pub, or a shop. In fact, you can never leave the house again, unless it's to have the jab. And if people find out you've avoided it they'll treat you like a leper, or like someone who avoided military conscription during the war, and shoot you at dawn.

So yes, it's compulsory.

Actually, I think I'll probably do my own vaccine tests. I'll get Doris to have it first and, if she's still alive and antler-free after a month, I might risk it.

20th December

Another announcement.

London's just gone into Tier 3. I think that's basically so that politicians don't have to go to work. And I suppose it's also harder to lynch them from two metres away.

Boris stopped just short of telling us we couldn't have Christmas any more. I guess nobody wants to be the bloke that cancels Christmas. It's not exactly a vote-winner.

That reminds me. I don't remember seeing a John Lewis advert this year. Perhaps there was one, but it didn't attract the hype of previous years. I suspect, like so many retail outlets, they're struggling.

21st December

More Covid restrictions.

Bank robbers have now been told that they must wear a mask when they're working. I suppose the hope is that they will instinctively disobey the law and get caught.

22nd December

Brexit negotiations are now reaching their final few hours, and things are getting tense.

France is threatening to send an Armada to steal our fish. Where's Lord Nelson when you need him?

Probably in London, standing on a column. Or perhaps he's been toppled by now by BLM activists. But to be fair, Nelson isn't as white as he looks – it's mainly pigeon shit.

I just heard a bloke from the EU called Guy Verhofstadt say one of the daftest things I've ever heard. "The UK want us to eat their fish," he ranted, "but how can we do that if we can't catch them?"

Well, knob-head - you buy them, obviously.

Perhaps I should be negotiating on behalf of the UK. It'd all be over by now.

23rd December

According to the news there's now a new strain of the virus, because the last one wasn't scaring us enough.

Apparently, new strains of viruses happen all the time, but this one is particularly important because we discovered it, and it's given France the excuse they needed to close their borders.

Ironic actually, as the new variant was first discovered in Kent.

Can't imagine how it got to Kent. Possibly via France, on a dinghy. Who knows?

Bottom line is, there's now about a thousand foreign lorry drivers stranded in Kent who can't get home, and God knows how many more foreigners inside the back of the lorries themselves.

Observers also spotted a French warship in our waters. Sounds like it's all going to kick off.

24th December

It's Christmas Eve now, and there's strong rumours of a Brexit trade deal being signed.

That's worrying. The only Brexit deal I'd trust is one that the EU wouldn't agree to.

So, if they're happy with this one, it basically means that we haven't read it carefully enough.

We've probably offered them lifelong ownership of every fish and chip shop in Britain, but to save face and satisfy the scrutiny of Nigel Farage, we were allowed to say that we still control a small portion of mushy peas.

Anyway, it's fish and chips for me tonight, as it happens, so I've just asked Doris to keep her eyes peeled for any foreigners behind the counter.

Dead giveaway.

25th December

Christmas falls on a Friday this year, which I think is a bit unfair.

Working folk get a few days off in lieu, but because I don't work I'm effectively missing out on that perk. It's basically a form of unemployment prejudice and it needs sorting.

Anyway, Merry Christmas.

Doris is popping round later with my turkey dinner. She decorated my tree last week and it looks glorious. On my suggestion, she managed to feed the cable from the tree lights into a long extension and in through her kitchen window, so she pays for the electric. It's only fair, as she works - otherwise all the electricity money would have to come out of my benefits, and that would eventually have to come out of her taxes.

Doris wasn't totally convinced at first, because she actually worked out once that she gets about £195 a week less than I do on benefits, despite her having three jobs. I had to point out though that the system's fair, because she has far less free time on her hands than me, so she doesn't really have much chance to shop, so the extra money would be wasted on her. I told her, it's no fun being stuck at home all day with nothing to buy. Frankly, I doubt she'd cope.

But apart from all that, they're also her lights, so not really my responsibility.

I've just watched the Queen's speech. I notice she wasn't wearing a mask. That's not setting a great example, but I suppose it's a bit awkward when it muffles your voice on the telly. Actually, I bet the Queen has quite a fancy mask, with a royal insignia on it, to cover the royal mouth and the royal nose. And perhaps Prince Andrew has a similar one, but without the identifying royal marks, so he can slip in and out of wealthy friends' houses incognito and without breaking sweat.

The rest of the TV schedule for Christmas looks a bit crap to be honest. There's no sign of 'The Great Escape', which is a shame because I was hoping to watch it so I could spot where Doris had gone so badly wrong with her plan.

So now it's a toss-up between Mrs Brown's Boys, which is about as funny as getting your nipple trapped in the zip of a hoodie, and repeats of Tipping Point, usually starring thick 'celebrities' who are slightly less famous than my uncle Pete, who's now dead but was once a Bingo-caller at Pontins.

Anyway, I'll wait for Doris to come round later so she can change the channel.

26th December

Boxing Day. A chance to put my feet up.

It was a busy day yesterday. I had the turkey to eat, plus the pudding and starter, (but not in that order) and Doris was late collecting all the used crockery. In the end I had to ring her and put in a reminder. I shouldn't really need to, but she can be a bit scatty sometimes and I know she had a lot on, so I felt I had to do my bit to get her back on track.

God knows what time she eventually finished the washing up. It wasn't just mine – she also had her own to do, and from what I hear Jack never lifts a finger to help. None of my business, of course, but if he was my husband I'd soon have a word.

Laziness is not an attractive quality in a bloke.

27th December

When I woke up I was under six inches of snow. Well, not me, thankfully, but the house.

That'll be another job for Doris. If she doesn't clear the path properly she might end up slipping when she comes to visit. And we all remember what happened with her last slip on the bag of frozen peas - a badly sprained ankle and weeks of lost productivity - so she really needs to make it a priority.

It's heavy work, but it's for her own good.

28th December

Doris slipped today while clearing the path and bruised her hip.

I didn't like to go on, but it just goes to prove my point. If she'd done it when I first pointed it out yesterday it wouldn't have been frozen underneath. But no, she said she couldn't do it in the dark, and she needed to be at work for half six the next morning, so it would have to wait until she got back. And now, of course, she's paying the price. I also notice Jack never offered to help.

29th December

Apparently, according to Doris, the Oxford vaccine has now been approved.

This is good news, because there's no way I'm having a foreign body penetrating my system. You never know what they've put in there, or if they've washed their hands.

I feel a bit happier with Oxford, because it's where Morse comes from. And Stephen Hawkeye as well I think. Both clever blokes. And Churchill. Although I think they're also all dead. But to be fair, that's probably a coincidence and nothing to do with the vaccine.

I think that I'm about tenth on the list of priorities for vaccinating. They start with the old folk in care homes and the care workers, then go down the age groups and rank people in terms of how vital their job is. Clearly they don't perceive my job as vital enough to receive any special consideration. A benefit claimant, they'd argue, is not a key worker.

It's a bit short-sighted, I think. Without benefit claimants, there'd be no benefits, and then what sort of society would we be? Also, without benefits claimants, all the people in Job Centres would have to be made redundant, and start claiming benefits. But where the hell would they go to claim them? Chaos.

Anyway, as it happens I'm in no rush to get jabbed, Oxford or not.

And to be honest, I can't imagine any self-respecting virus wanting to hang around inside my body. It might catch something.

30th December

It's New Year's Eve soon, so they say on the news.

Well, good riddance to 2020. It's been a total bastard. The virus, the cancelled shows, the pubs shut, Doris's ankle – it's been a total nightmare.

Then, of course, there was her house flooding, some of which seeped through to my wall. I had to ask a man to come and examine my damp patch. And it's been a long time since I last did that.

Anyway, I've just caught up on the latest, and Boris has announced that every pub in the world, except three on the Scilly Isles, have got to shut tonight.

This comes, bear in mind, on the afternoon before New Year's Eve, when thousands of pubs have just booked in record numbers of customers, bought shit-loads of food, stocked up on extra beer and arranged staffing.

Meanwhile, three pubs on the Isles of Scilly, plus the local ferry, have just taken 58 million last-minute bookings and need extra help. The words 'piss up' and 'brewery' spring to mind.

31st December

It's been confirmed on the BBC news - it's New Year's Eve tonight.

Usually during the working week I go to bed around nine, but on special occasions like this I'll stay up till more like half past nine, just to let the New Year in.

I can always have a lie-in tomorrow to compensate.

31st December - midnight

I can't sleep.

I've been trying quite hard, and I was, until recently, having some success, but then the noisy bastards next door started letting off fireworks at some ungodly hour.

I can guarantee that means the next-door neighbour's dog will have shat himself again all over my lawn. It took ages for Doris to clean it up last time.

It's not her dog, it's the other next-door neighbour's, so I couldn't really be too annoyed with her, but even so it's a nuisance.

I've reset my alarm for 3pm and, just to play extra safe, switched it off.

1st January 2021

The Isles of Scilly have just gone into Tier 5.

This was unexpected and, as a consequence, hundreds of people with woolly jumpers and beards have been arrested following an illegal rave at three of its pubs.

It's New Year's Day.

Shame, really. 2020 was such a good year.

I'm joking, of course. 2020 was the annual equivalent of Hitler. What did the Queen call it once when she had that really crap year in 1992?

Her "Anus Horribilis" or something like that.

I looked it up on Wankepedia and I think that's the Latin

for 'horrible arse', and she was right. 1992 was the year that three of her kids' marriages went tits up, and her Windsor Castle home went up in flames.

Not great, admittedly, but really not in the same league as 2020 when it comes to horrible arse years. After all, 2020 was the year that probably every marriage in the country went tits up at some point, along with their businesses, individual freedoms, holidays, jobs, lifestyles, our mental and physical health, law and order, our future, any real sense of proportion, objective truth and decency, and all our hopes and dreams.

Apart from that, it went quite well.

If 1992 was an 'anus horribilis' then surely 2020 was a 'cuntus maximus'. Though to be fair I can't really imagine the Queen saying that on telly.

I'm a great admirer of HMV The Queen, or to give her her full and proper title, Elizabeth Vagina. That's also Latin. Useful language, Latin. I brushed up on a couple of Latin phrases one idle Sunday, because you never know when you might meet a dead Roman, though I guess that's less likely now we've left the EU.

Oh, yes, nearly forgot to mention that.

Apparently we officially left the EU at eleven o'clock last night, while I was asleep. So I guess it's now a case of welcome aboard HMS The United Kingdom.

It's been a stormy passage so far, lots of in-fighting with the crew, and there's no doubt more rough seas ahead. But the journey is now underway, so I just hope that those still aboard now decide to climb to new heights to help mend a sail or fly a flag, rather than just skulking below deck drilling little holes in the hull. Whether you wanted it or not, it's happened. Don't try and sink your own vessel to prove a point.

Anyway, that's enough ship analogies for now. The sun's well over the yard arm, so I'm going to have a glass of rum. Nautical, but nice.

5th January

Boris has just announced another major list of restrictions.

From now on, everybody has to be locked in a lead casket from 6pm until midnight. You're allowed one toilet break a week, on a Wednesday, and you can see your support bubble for twenty minutes a month through a telescope, provided they're covered in bubble-wrap.

Food is allowed, as long as you wash it thoroughly before you eat it. I did put my bag of crisps under the tap, but they weren't as nice as normal.

To be fair to Boris though, I've decided that being the Prime Minister is a shit job. Whatever you do, everybody hates you – either for doing it, or for not doing it quick enough.

I reckon if I was Prime Minister (and you never know) I'd not even try to please everybody. I'd just concentrate on doing something really amazing for about half a dozen people, and then tell the rest to fuck off. That way, I'd have about half a dozen less people hating me than Boris has.

Those six votes could be vital. Because, let's be honest, nobody really likes the other Labour bloke either – the one who looks like a startled rabbit and kneels down a lot.

In fact, come to think of it, does anybody like any politician at all, ever? Why on earth do they do that job? Is it because they crave the power to piss people off in bulk? Is it to get a free second house? Or is it perhaps just to get on Strictly?

When I'm Prime Minister, things will change, probably mainly for the worse, but at least we'll all know where we stand.

When I'm there at the Covid 27 press conference and Robert Pisston, or whatever his name is, asks me one of his long, rambling questions laced throughout with thinly-veiled smarmy criticism, I'll just reply: "Thanks for the question, Robert, but I'm afraid you bored the tits off me halfway through the first sentence and I wasn't listening – let's go to the next slide..."

6th January

Strange day.

I noticed a nasty red rash had appeared on my arms, so Doris took me to the doctors. Turned out it wasn't as bad as I first thought. The rash was tiny spots of dried-on tomato ketchup.

Apparently I'd shaken the bottle so vigorously last night trying to get the stuff to come out onto my sausage that I'd covered myself.

It was a close call though - the doctor only twigged what was going on when Doris happened to mention that she'd noticed the rash had spread to my kitchen ceiling. The doctor said that was unusual, and did a biopsy. Well, not so much a biopsy as such – he just took a scraping and tasted it, so I got the results back straight away.

Why on earth these sauce-bottle folk can't make the stuff come out easier I don't know. It took Doris hours to wipe down the walls.

Thankfully, she took full responsibility, because she'd cooked the sausage, but not everybody is lucky enough to have such an honest neighbour.

7th January

I just heard today that the first of my newly-scheduled Revolution shows has been cancelled yet again by the Walsall Forest Arts Centre. Originally it was supposed to have happened last spring. And, having already delayed the performance by a year, the vaccine was seen as the best hope of ensuring that the show eventually went on. But, by a terrible twist of irony, I'm now told I can't put the show this time either, because the venue has now been commandeered by Walsall Council as a main vaccination centre.

Can't do the show without a vaccine. Can't do the show *because* of a vaccine. You couldn't make it up.

I also read that they're vaccinating people twice – the main one and then a booster one a few weeks later.

That strikes me as a total waste of time and resources.

I wonder if anybody's thought about using a bigger syringe and shoving it all in at once? It cuts down on travelling. Otherwise it's a bit like having to go to the takeaway twice – once for the fish, another time for the chips.

Good job vaccines don't also need mushy peas, otherwise that'd be three trips. Ludicrous. It's all mixed up when it's in your stomach anyway.

And of course with my system the needle itself needn't be any bigger, so it wouldn't hurt any more than a normal dose. Just pop the two liquids together, give them a quick stir in a saucepan or whatever, and bingo, job done.

That's the trouble with scientists. They might be really clever with chemicals and stuff, but they often display no common sense, and can't even tie their own shoelaces.

Doris once went out with a scientist. Well, I say scientist – I think he actually made sausages, which is a fairly similar skill-set: mixing ingredients, testing them out on people, seeing if they died, etc. But when it came to practical stuff he was hopeless, so she chucked him and married Jack instead. Jack knows how to mend a hairdryer and how to stop taps from dripping, which is ultimately all you need from a bloke.

8th January

I asked Doris about her scientist friend.

Apparently he was a scientologist, which is something a bit different. He did work at the local butchers though, making sausages. And she chucked him because she said he was a bit weird. "Off his yed." I think she said. "A bit like Tom Cruise."

I must say, I don't think I would have chucked a boyfriend who was a bit like Tom Cruise. But that's Doris for you – she's never had any taste in men. I'm sure Jack would be the first to admit it.

9th January

I've just seen a very disturbing video on Facebook.

About six police with stab vests were arresting an 80 year old woman for sitting on a park bench in the fresh air on her own.

Meanwhile, in the background unnoticed, three blokes were robbing the bank with machetes and machine guns. But apparently they weren't breaking the law because they had masks on.

The police have since issued a statement apologising to the robbers, because the bank staff didn't always stay two metres back, and have invited them to come forward to put in a claim for compensation.

The old woman, meanwhile, who's thought to be a militant librarian, is being sentenced at the Old Bailey next Tuesday, charged with sitting on a bench in a way likely to cause uniformed people with no sense of proportion to arrest her.

Thank goodness we don't live in a police state, like North Korea or Scotland. In fact, perhaps it's something about folk in the north generally?

Although I suppose that wouldn't account for the Met Police. Or Wales. Or Dorset, which is where the bench woman was.

No, in fact, bollocks to that theory.

It's probably nothing to do with the north. After all, compared to Jack, who's a Brummie, I'm from the north myself, but I don't make a habit of arresting octogenarian bench-dwellers.

To give them the benefit of the doubt, though, I'm assuming that the police on the video were just acting on explicit instructions from their bosses. And who knows, they might be from the north. Or Scottish. Or both.

10th January

With Doris being off duty, no washing is being done, and I'm having to wear the same clothes every day.

I do take a pride in my smell, and it worries me that after thirteen days in the same undies it might eventually start causing body odour.

I was reading up on this and apparently you can't smell it yourself, especially if you've got the virus, but other people and wildlife can. I say wildlife, because the bloke over the road has a bloodhound, and I noticed yesterday he was taking it to the vet because it had passed out.

Hopefully that's not my fault, but I had just recently opened my window, and I did hear him whimpering just before he rolled over, so you never know. I'm not a great fan of dogs generally, but I don't like to see them suffering unnecessarily.

Anyway, as a precaution, I'm going to go to the clothes bank tomorrow and see what's available in a size medium.

11th January

The clothes bank was shut.

More virus red tape. The caretaker bloke there said they're now having to fumigate everything before anybody else can wear it. I asked him if he could fumigate my stuff, but he said it was impossible unless I took it off first, so I went home empty-handed.

12th January

A nice surprise tonight.

Quite a few NHS nurses live in our street, and Doris arranged for them to stand outside at 8pm and clap for me, as I've been such a good customer over the years.

I noticed the miserable bugger at number 16 didn't come out though. Doris said she might have been on a night shift, but I reckon she just used that as an excuse. She knows how to hold a grudge, that one, and she probably still blames me for pole-axing her husband's bloodhound last week. Doris says he had to have steroids and be put on a drip. The dog - not the husband. They clocked up a four hundred and fifty quid vet's bill. Crazy. You can probably buy a brand new dog for that much – one with nothing wrong with it.

Our Trojan (my eldest) wanted to be a vet once, but she

said it involved too much studying. I suppose it's a bit like being a doctor, except it's a lot easier to get to see a vet.

I remember when Doris fell down the stairs last year and fractured her leg. She waited six hours at the hospital in agony – in the end Jack took her to the vets. They got an X-ray sorted in ten minutes. That's always her first port of call now if she feels a bit dodgy. In fact, I think she's currently on tablets for distemper. Doris says it can be a bit expensive, but I think Jack's got her on some sort of Pet Plan insurance for so much a month.

13th January

Boris has just banned some flights into the UK.

The idea is to try and keep out the riff-raff – especially any riff-raff with new strains of Covid. I think we've got enough on our plate without inviting new variants in. I know variety is the spice of life, but a brand new Covid germ with extra vigour that sticks two fingers up to the vaccine and laughs haughtily is probably something we could all do without.

To be honest, I don't know why Boris didn't ban all flights into the UK a bit earlier than this, like around 1970. It might have saved quite a few issues over the years.

If we'd had a policy of outgoing flights only for around forty or fifty years, then bit by bit there'd have been more benefit payments to go round, fewer food banks, and less pressure on the NHS. And, of course, no viruses.

Obviously I realise that Boris wasn't in charge in 1970, so it's probably not all his fault. In fact, I've just looked it up, and he was only six at the time, so he's off the hook.

According to Wankepedia, the Prime Minister back then was a bloke called Edward Heath. I remember him well. Big teeth, liked sailing his private yacht, playing the piano (badly) and conducting orchestras (equally badly) and his shoulders went up and down a lot when he laughed. Or at least Mike Yarwood's shoulders went up and down a lot when he was impersonating him (also badly).

Actually, some of you might be too young to remember Mike Yarwood. When I was a kid he was the country's finest impersonator, from a choice of one.

January 14th

I decided to have a go on this new social media craze,

TikTok is bizarre. Full of precocious pre-pubescent girls from exotic places like Taiwan, pouting, dancing, miming and singing into their hairbrush like they've got their own TV show. Pop culture at its most trashy and irrelevant.

Anyway, you've got to try these things to keep up with 'the kids' so I posted a few little clips of me swearing a lot at a nettle, and managed to get a handful of followers, mostly from Taiwan.

January 15th

I mentioned my TikTok experience to Doris, and she reckons, that Jack reckons, that TikTok is basically a spying tool to allow the Chinese to steal all your data.

To be honest, that sort of thing doesn't really bother me.

As far as I know, I haven't got any data. And even if I have, the Chinese are welcome to it. If they can use my bank details, Job Centre sign-on days and NHS records to their advantage then good luck to them, because I certainly can't.

I also can't understand why Jack is so paranoid about that sort of thing. You'd have to be seriously bored to spy on Jack. No offence to Doris's husband, but Jack's life is not really the sort of thing that James Bond films are made of.

There are some exciting Jacks out there – Jack Nicholson, Jack Lemmon, Jack Black, Jack Sparrow, Jack Spratt, Jack the Ripper, and that bloke up the beanstalk – but my neighbour, sadly, isn't one of them.

His Viking name would have probably been something like Jack the Boring, had he been interesting enough to have been a Viking, which he isn't.

He's also, thankfully, too boring to read my book.

January 16th

Wolves lost again. To West Bromwich Albion. Twats.

January 17th

Doris has now gone into a major depression, because she supports the Wolves and Jack supports the Albion.

Well, when I say support, they've never been anywhere near a football match. Actually, I think Jack went to a game once when he was about six, although to hear him talk you'd think he was a lifelong season ticket holder with WBA tattooed on his brow.

It's too expensive anyway. To go to a premiership match now you need to be as rich as a premiership footballer, which is ironic because they get in for free. In fact, it's probably cheaper to cut out the middle-man and just buy your favourite player a new Ferrari every week.

The only thing I know about football is that Steve Bull used to play for the Wolves. Steve's a good bloke. Born in Tipton. He also made a guest appearance in the Doreen movie a few years back, and I can confirm that, given the options of football or acting, he definitely made the right career choice.

January 18th

Dreams are weird.

I had a really bizarre one last night. I was in the garden, and out of a bush walks a tiny version of Lewis Hamilton, about two feet tall, holding a large cucumber, and he starts swearing at me.

Yes, I know you're now all waiting for the punchline, but there isn't one. That was it. But you have to ask yourself, why? Why did I dream that?

Yes, I'm sure the amateur psychoanalysts out there will all be chuntering "Oh, it's just the classic textbook miniature Formula One driver holding a cucumber and swearing dream.

Others who follow Freudian philosophy will point to the fact that it's a black man holding a large phallic symbol of fertility emerging from my bush, but I don't want to go there. I refuse to believe that my mind works that way. I think Lewis Hamilton might have been on the telly briefly last week, but so were lots of other people, like Piers Morgan and Boris Johnson, and they didn't emerge from a bush carrying a vegetable and start swearing at me – or if they did I have no memory of it.

I must stop eating cheese late at night – especially cheese and onion crisps.

I'll also get Doris to chuck that mouldy cucumber out of the fridge.

19th January

To pass the time I started writing a new kids' book.

It's called Poetry in my Ocean, and it's a collection of poems all about our oceans and the amazing creatures that live in there. I've been doing some research and unearthed some extraordinary facts.

Did you know, for example, that an octopus has eight legs? You probably did.

But what you possibly didn't know is that they also have nine brains. As well as their main brain, each leg has its own mini brain, which is great until each brain starts to have a different opinion about where to go. I often think it'd be a good idea if my two legs each had a brain.

Octopuses also have three hearts, blue blood, and no bones. Having no bones means they can squeeze into really tiny places, like the ocean.

19th January

I just did a phone interview on Gorgeous FM with a nice chap called Ric.

Apparently it's a gay radio station. I didn't realize radio stations could be gay, but nothing surprises me these days.

In fact, I didn't even think animals could be gay until I did some research for my new Revolution show (that's the show that feels like it's never going to happen because of lockdown) but the stuff I found out was a real eye-opener.

For example, did you know that bison actually have more gay sex than heterosexual sex? Course you didn't, unless you're a camp bison. That's because female bison only let the males mate with them about once a year, and that isn't enough for a typical red-blooded male bison. So during the mating season, out of sheer frustration, the males end up shagging each other several times a day.

It could be that they enjoy gay sex, or it could just be that they've got really crap eyesight. But either way, it's been calculated that more than 50% of 'mounting' in young bison males happens amongst the same gender.

Now, I don't know if you've ever mounted a male bison, (and just for the record, I haven't) but it's apparently not quite as easy as it sounds. But my advice is, if you do happen to mount one, even by accident, always remember to wash your hands afterwards, in the wash bison.

Meanwhile, I then discover that around one third of all albatrosses are lesbians. That sort of information is invaluable, but only if you happen to be an albatross.

Unlike some human lesbians, albatross lesbians usually tend to stay together for life, as it takes two parents to successfully rear a chick together. The chicks have often been fathered by males that are already in another committed relationship. I'm guessing that for a frisky male albatross, having a quick dabble with a lesbian is quite high up on the bucket list. Again, just like humans.

A fifth of all swans are gay.

I'm not sure how they measure these things by the way, but I found it on Wankepedia, so it must be true.

Like many birds, swans stick with one partner for years. But many of them choose a same-sex partner. In fact, gay swans often start families together, possibly to make them more appealing to the casting directors of TV adverts.

Male walruses, meanwhile, only reach sexual maturity at the age of four (which still sounds quite early to me, but walruses have different standards).

Until then, most of them are exclusively gay. Once they've reached maturity, they become bisexual – mating with females during the breeding season, while having sex with other males the rest of the year.

In short, walruses are sluts.

Sheep aren't much better. Studies suggest that even when fertile females are available, about 10% of males in flocks of sheep prefer to shag other males, especially if they're Welsh farmers.

However, strangely enough, this only occurs amongst domestic sheep, so we have to question if that counts as natural.

Studies also have found that gay sheep have a different brain structure from their heterosexual counterparts, and release fewer sex hormones. A bit like me.

But the award for the most gay sex goes to, believe it or not, giraffes. Gay sex accounts for more than 90% of all sexual activity in giraffes. But they don't just get straight to business. Male giraffes like to indulge in foreplay that can last for up to an hour. This, of course, is mainly necking.

So, as you can see, animals in their natural habitat can be LGB. But what about T? Is there such a thing as a trans animal? I had to know, so again I consulted Wankepedia.

The answer, amazingly, is yes – despite the fact that animals don't tend to use Twitter to show off their sexual preferences.

Some of the larger female Kobudai fish will suddenly go all moody, disappear under a rock for a few days, undergo a weird hormonal transformation where their body and head get much bigger, and then come back as a male. No doubt they then enter the Fish Olympics as females and win all the medals.

Actually, this sort of weird trans behaviour is actually quite common amongst fish. Clown fish are all born male and later turn into females. Obviously they all transition at different times, otherwise there'd be chaos in the changing rooms.

In the clown fish community, the female dominates, and prefers to have sex with a big man fish. If the female dies, then the dominant male will then automatically transition into a female. It's a pity we humans can't do the same – think how much it'd save the NHS.

Chickens can't really change gender, but apparently some chickens have been known to be half male and half female, which is obviously important if you prefer breasts to legs.

But the prize for this half and half gender trick surely must ultimately go to spotted hyenas, because (cue drum roll...) female hyenas have got a penis.

Yes, you heard me right. They have willies. In fact, hyenas are the only female mammals who copulate, urinate, and even give birth through their penis-like canal.

Christ, that must hurt. Giving birth through a penis. I'd like to see you blokes try that – see how we feel.

It's even possible, apparently, for females to get erections. In fact, hyenas have to "retract" their appendages into their body in order for a male to have sex with them. You have to ask - wouldn't it just be easier just to book a holiday in Thailand?

So there you have it.

The so-called natural world is full of apparently unnatural behaviour, so who are we to judge?

The motto here would seem to be – each to their own.

That's especially true of the female hyenas, who would appear to already have everything they need for a fun night in with the girls.

No wonder they're always loffin'.

20th January

It's Donald Trump's last day as President.

I haven't really been following the American news, but they must have finally finished counting all the votes they found in Joe Biden's loft, so he's being sworn in today.

It will be interesting to see how long it is before the new bloke is the baddie. I reckon about an hour.

21st January

Joe Biden has just announced his main policies.

As far as I can tell, Biden's policies are simply to reverse all of Trump's policies.

So if Trump says build the wall, Biden says un-build the wall. If Trump says play tough with China, Biden says play table-tennis with China. If Trump says do a trade deal with the UK, Biden says put us to the back of the queue.

It would've been interesting to see what Biden might have done if Trump had said 'Vote for Biden.' Biden would then probably have retaliated with 'Don't vote for Biden' and confused all his followers, which consist of the media, Hollywood Stars and the imaginary people in his loft who voted for him by post.

When he finally runs out of Trump policies to reverse, I reckon Biden should take on Trump as a special adviser, and ask him what not to do next.

There's talk of impeaching Trump, mainly to make sure he can never be the President again. If I were Trump I would encourage this. It will confuse Biden and possibly cause him to oppose it. I sometimes think I should have gone into politics. Doris says I'm too politically incorrect. I say that's bollocks.

28th January

Not been sleeping too well lately.

Couldn't settle, and was tossing and turning all afternoon. I mentioned this to Doris and she's lent me a new CD to listen to, which she says might help.

It's designed for people doing Yoga, and it's supposed to help you relax and put your mind into a tranquil state. Can't imagine it working with me, but the telly's boring again, so I think I might pop it on now and have a quick listen.

29th January

Just woke up on the rug. Don't know what happened.

30th January

I just discovered that I didn't wake up on the 29th January after all. According to the news it's now the 30th. That means I lost about a day and a half, thanks to that CD. I might pop it on again tonight.

2nd February

It seems to have worked again.

If anything, it was better than last time. The key to curing insomnia seems to be getting plenty of sleep. I need to get Doris to move the CD player into my bedroom though. Waking up on the floor is doing my back in.

5th February

I've been talked into doing my first live-stream tonight.

It's a bit scary, to be honest, being live – though I suppose it's better than being dead. I'm having to use Doris's wifi, which is a lot better than mine, mainly because I haven't got any. My wifi is basically Doris's wifi but with a wall in-between, which makes it less efficient, so she's going to run some sort of cable through the tunnel she made into my kitchen and plug it directly into my laptop. Well, when I say my laptop – it's actually Doris's laptop, which she's lending me.

I don't have a computer and I don't really understand it all, but apparently all I've got to do is talk for an hour, which I think I can manage.

Tonight's more about testing the equipment and seeing if anybody actually bothers to listen.

I'll report back.

9pm

Well, I'm told we had thousands listening, including some from abroad.

There were folks from Spain, America, and even Dubai. Not sure if they even speak English in Dubai. But I don't suppose it matters, given that I don't speak English either.

Anyway, on the strength of that, we'll be doing another live-stream next Saturday, as it's Valentine's weekend.

I've asked Doris to knock me up a quiz to keep folks amused in lockdown. She's on a triple shift today, but I expect she'll get down to it when she gets home. And the most exciting news of all is, the lovely Joe Lycett has agreed to come online and have a chat with me.

10th February

I've just been chatting to Joe Lycett.

What a lovely chap, despite being a Brummie.

He seems to be on just about every TV programme going at the moment – Would I Lie to You, QI, The One Show, Live at the Apollo, Eight out of Ten Cats, The Graham Norton Show, Sewing Bee, Taskmaster and quite a few others – I wouldn't even be surprised if he popped up on Question Time. So it was good of him to take the time to appear on my Cheap and Cheerful TV effort.

We were using a high tech video link, which neither of us really understood, and as far as I'm aware this was the first time in recorded history that somebody from the Black Country has actually communicated directly with somebody from the distant alien constellation of Brum.

There was a bit of dodgy echo delay on Joe's mike, which is understandable as he was on totally different planet, but otherwise it went quite well.

I even managed to sing him a love song, which you can possibly find on MyTube, if you could be arsed.

13th February

It's the day of the Valentine's livestream.

I put out a message on Faceache to see if anybody wanted to join me live on the show to propose to their partner. No takers.

But I did have two blokes who wanted to come on air to ask for a divorce, which I thought was quite touching.

I have to say, I was a bit wary about doing this Valentine's show, because what inevitably happens at an event like that is that all the blokes watching take a bit of a fancy to me, and then it all kicks off with their partners and ends in tears.

Now, obviously I don't want that to happen on Valentine's night, so I decided that I needed to take certain steps to try and de-emphasise my natural sexuality.

Jack agreed that I'd done a pretty good job.

It was basically just clever use of make-up, i.e. avoiding it, pulling up the zip that little bit higher on my hoodie, and making my hair less sexily windswept and alluring.

It all helps to calm the natural male urges, apparently. I needed to try and be less of a sexy kitten, and more of a poxy cougar.

How you present yourself is, of course, important, but in my experience, the best contraception you can have is a strong Black Country accent.

Anyway, I go live at 8pm again, and I doubt we'll finish much before bedtime, so I'll report back tomorrow.

14th February

Happy Valentine's Day.

It went well, I think. Just the one offer of marriage, but I think he was taking the piss to be honest. For a start he was clearly gay, and I reckon he'd had about seventeen pints. In the end, his wife had to call the police.

Joe Lycett was also good last night – in fact, just as good as he was when we pre-recorded him. Doris did a pretty good job with the quiz as well, as it happens. She found out some really interesting facts about Valentine's Day to base all the questions on. For example, did you know that the phrase "wearing your heart on your sleeve" comes from the Middle Ages?

Blokes would choose their partners while attending a Roman festival honouring Juno, and after choosing, the men literally then wore the names of the women on their sleeves to show their bond during the festivities. It was a bit like having a tattoo, only less permanent, and also less embarrassing when you chuck 'em a month later.

I also learnt that the Valentine's Day tradition of giving a box of chocolates was started in the 19th century by… guess who? Yep. It was a bloke called Cadbury. Well he fucking would, wouldn't he. Bloody Brummies.

Another quick historical fact - one of the most romantic things to ever happen on Valentine's Day was the Saint Valentine's Day Massacre in 1929, when seven members of Chicago's North Side Gang were gathered at a Lincoln Park garage, lined up against a wall and shot with machine guns. They left a little note which read: 'Al Capone sends his love.'

15th February

Christ, it's cold.

It was minus seven here last night, and I had to go to bed still wearing my hoodie. But that's nothing compared to Scotland.

Doris reckons it went down to minus twenty-three in the Highlands a week or two ago. Yes, minus twenty-three. That means that Scotland was officially about five degrees colder than a fridge freezer. Imagine that in a kilt. The slightest knock and your genitals would fall off.

It was the lowest temperature recorded in the UK for over a quarter of a century. And that worries me. If it can be this cold when we're suffering from global warming, what's it going to be like when we all start driving electric cars and ban coal? What's the point in saving the planet from over-heating if we all freeze to death?

I just hope that these scientists know what they're doing. Trouble is, just lately they seem to be proving on a daily basis that they don't.

Of course, it does all benefit the energy industries. Being locked down at home in bleak mid-winter means their profits are going through the roof (quite literally if you've got no loft insulation). But at least they've done their little bit to help, by announcing another price increase.

Twats. That's just what the country needs. Higher energy bills when small businesses are on their arse and nobody can work.

Thank God I'm self-sufficient in energy. I persuaded Doris to let me run a couple of extension cables into her house, as I'm unemployed, so at least my little array of fan heaters, and my plasma, hoover, hairdryer and kettle don't cost me anything. I suppose we all have to do our bit to save the planet.

Anyway, it's actually Doris that sticks the kettle on when she's round here cleaning, so it's technically her that using the electricity the most.

Only fair then that she makes a small contribution to the cost, by paying for it all.

16th February

I just read that Donald Trump has been acquitted on his impeachment trial.

Actually, I think that's the second time they've tried to impeach him. Probably won't be the last. I'm not sure you can impeach people for just playing golf, being orange and owning hotels, but they'll keep trying.

I wonder if, like a certain Arnold Schwarzenegger, he'll be back?

22nd February

So, Boris has finally announced a road map to get us out of lockdown.

I've never been very good at reading maps, because I'm a woman, but it seems to suggest that the kids will go back to school in a couple of weeks (providing the teachers' unions don't kick off) and all restrictions will be lifted by June 21st, which ironically is the longest day of the year.

Actually, it's good that the teachers get to go back for a week or two before they break up for summer. It'll remind them where they work.

Talking about work, it now looks like my rescheduled Revolution tour is officially screwed again. It was due to end on the 19th June, just two days before restrictions are probably now going to end. I'll have one last go at getting it rescheduled for autumn.

23rd February

To celebrate the end of lockdown, and because (thanks to Boris's roadmap) I've now officially got bugger all else to do, I've decided to write a little pop song.

I started tinkering on Doris's piano (I made her disinfect the keys first) and came up with a very catchy little tune.

Though I say it myself, in pure musical terms it's quite a sophisticated composition, because it employs two more chords than any Status Quo single ever written. In other words, five.

I'm going to call it Lockdown Baby.

I'm hoping I can get it into the download charts, but I'm not holding my breath, as it requires the good people of the Black Country who follow me to part with a quid, and they only tend to do that if there's a scratchcard involved, or better still a kebab.

I'll now apply the acid test for music - if I'm still whistling this tune tomorrow, I'll start writing some lyrics for it.

24th February

I can't remember the tune.

Luckily though, Doris can. She says it stuck in her head and she couldn't sleep last night. I told her it didn't stick in my head and I could sleep last night, but nevertheless her positive reaction has encouraged me to pursue it, so I have now started scribbling down some lyrics.

One lyric from the chorus I wrote said: "Come for me, Doris – lock me right down…" Doris says that sounded rude. It wasn't meant that way, but Doris is strange about things like that, and says she doesn't want to be part of the song, which is a shame because it scanned and rhymed quite nicely.

But I've now had a flash of genius after watching the BBC news, and changed it to "Come for me, Boris – lock me right down…" which I think is even better. And it doesn't matter if people think it's rude any more, because that's the sort of thing Boris does, allegedly.

My lawyer told me to write allegedly there, just in case. Not sure what difference it makes, to be honest, because the only one alleging it is probably me. And I'm not even sure what I'm alleging. I just liked the sound of the words.

1st March

Started recording the new single today.

It was an interesting experience. They made me dress up in leather, so I looked like a rock chick. Actually, probably more a chicken than a chick. And they told me I needed to put on some lipstick. It's been a long time since I did that. So long, in fact, that I couldn't even remember where you're supposed to put it, until the producer pointed out there was a clue in the name lipstick.

"There's a mirror in the toilet," he said. He still didn't specify which end of the body you're supposed to apply it to though, so I hope I did the right thing.

First day at the studio was tiring. Scantily-clad, I had to sing the same line over and over again, while they pointed microphones and cameras at me from various angles. Nothing below waist height though, so the whole lipstick saga was a waste of time.

Apparently, it's all because sex sells records.

The producers spent several hours whispering up a corner, apparently deciding how best to turn me into a latter-day Marilyn Monroe.

 I didn't really catch all of the conversation, but I did overhear one of them ask the make-up lady if there was a better way to cover up all my wrinkles.

She replied: "Yes, use a tarpaulin." Bitch.

Anyway, I was knackered when I got home, and Doris had to interrupt her own tea to come and cook mine. I've got three more days of this before the record's completed.

I did ask Doris if she wanted to be on backing vocals. Apparently she was in the choir at school, and does a belting karaoke version of Delilah when she's pissed.

That's good enough for me.

2nd March

On my recommendation, the producer invited Doris along to the studio to have a go at the backing vocals.

He didn't seem very impressed. In fact, he told her to come back when she's pissed, and when he's next recording a cover version of Delilah.

He told me afterwards, in private, that it's not that Doris can't sing, it's just that she can't sing in a way that's likely to cause any pleasure to humans. That seemed a bit harsh, but I suppose he knows what he's doing. After all, he gave her a fair trial, and she was found guilty.

But I also felt a bit guilty about putting Doris through such an embarrassing ordeal, and I wanted to do something to make it up to her – a token gesture. The local petrol station does daffodils for a quid, so I got Doris to pick me up a bunch on her way back from work and then, the moment she gave to them to me, I handed them straight back, as a surprise, saying "These are for you." Well, you should have seen her face. It was all blotchy. To be fair, I never even knew that Doris was allergic to daffodils.

No problem, though. I kept them myself in the end, and Doris said not to worry about the quid, so it was all sorted.

We had a good laugh about it later. Well, I did. Doris was concentrating on her breathing.

3rd March

The final day of recording the single and the promotional video.

God knows how they're going to edit it all. Three days, cut down to three minutes. I think I did eighteen takes of one note, trying to get it in tune. In the end, I heard one of them say they would use that note somewhere else, where it didn't have to be that note.

I thought I was quite a good singer, but it's much harder to do when somebody's listening. Hard for them, too.

Same problem with the video. It's quite good until you start looking at it. But there's quite a lot of technical wizardry here at the studio, so I reckon they'll be doing something clever in the editing and replace my body with somebody else's – preferably female and attractive.

They did pluck up courage to ask me about doing a semi-nude scene. I told them to sod off. The producer said: "Don't worry - we'll find a body double."

The make-up lady then chimed in with: "Where are we going to find a whale at this short notice?"

And that's when I finally punched her. She'd been asking for it all week.

If the make-up lady ever needs a body double, they'll need to find a peroxide blonde with a flat nose, black eye and a dislocated jaw, so good luck with that.

On the whole though, I'm really looking forward to the single being released. It's been an incredibly fast and furious journey, from idly tinkling Doris's piano ivories just over a week ago, to now recording the finished article. Release date is set to be second week of March.

Will it make it into the download charts? Time will tell.

4th March

The single has been released – earlier than planned. I think that's to make sure it's still topical, given that the kids are going back to school on Monday, and by then it won't feel so much like a lockdown.

5th March

On early evidence, I don't think I'll be ordering my pop star's yacht anytime soon.

So far, after 24 hours, about 8 people have downloaded the track. That's 7,992 short of my target of 8000, which is what I'm told you need to get into the download charts.

To be fair, everybody seemed to like it, but the dilemma of the modern world of social media is that in order to sell something, you have to show it to them first. In the case of music, that means they get to listen before they buy. And if they can listen online, any time they want, why bother buying it? Nobody's quite sorted that problem out yet.

Apparently, these days everybody rents their music and listens to it on something called Spotify, which then pays the artist every time their track is played.

Sounds good. Except for the fact that what they actually pay is (and I'm not joking here) around one hundredth of a dollar for every play. So after a year, if my single proves popular, I might get a dollar, which is not enough for a yacht. Minus VAT of course. And minus the distributor's commission. And after 30% overseas tax has been withheld because I'm not an American.

Next time I do a single, if there is a next time, I don't think I'll bother with any downloads, I'll just have one vinyl copy made, and raffle it off as a collector's item.

6th March

I got a letter today asking me to book my Covid jab.

It's a bit of a dilemma, because I was intending to wait for Doris to have hers – partly so she could give me a lift, and partly so I could see if she grew any antlers or had any other side effects. But Doris is younger than me, so I could end up waiting a long time.

So anyway, I came up with an ingenious plan. Doris can book the appointment for me, using all my data, and then turn up instead of me and get jabbed. Once I know she's okay, I'll tell the authorities that she stole my identity so I can have my own jab.

I reckon that Doris will get off with a caution, so no harm done. Best to play safe.

7th March

Doris doesn't seem too keen on the stolen identity idea.

Some days I don't know what to make of that woman. I think it's probably Jack filling her head with all sorts of practical nonsense, like how would he cope if she went to prison?

To be fair, if Doris did go to prison it would be me that suffered more so than Jack. He can look after himself.

8th March

The kids go back to school today.

The UK is suddenly full of depressed teachers. But never mind – in a couple of weeks it'll be Easter, so they can have another few months off.

There's actually been some talk of the Government trying to shorten the summer holidays to help kids catch up on many months of lost learning.

Good luck with that.

Ironically, the kids will probably be up for it, and so will the parents. But I suspect, after such a long and stressful lay-off from the daily rigours of the school classroom, the teachers will need their rest.

Strange old world.*

*Quick update on this – I just saw on social media that the teachers unions had voted on plans to either extend school hours or shorten the summer holiday in order to catch up.

The vote went 10% in favour, 90% against.

I'm in shock. Didn't see that coming.

9th March

There's a big interview on Oprah tonight with Meghan and Harry.

I've decided to record my own little social media tribute to it. I'll play Meghan myself. I've got a black dress, and I can make it look like a seagull's shit on it, which I think is the effect Meghan was going for on her designer outfit.

Unfortunately, I can't be in two places at once so I can't play Harry as well, but I do have a puppet I can use, and a ginger wig to stick on it.

I'll report back.

10th March

I'm in shock again.

There were over half a million views for my Meghan and Harry video. And around another 200,000 views for the shorter TikTok version. Plus Twitter views of 80,000.

It seems to have captured the public mood.

12th March

I'm not happy with the amount of exercise I'm getting in lockdown. It's far too much.

Doris doesn't agree, but I'm afraid that Doris is biased. Also, Doris - despite being a lovely lady and a wonderful neighbour - isn't really bright enough to understand the theory of relativity.

Allow me to explain.

You see, according to a bloke called Einstein (who, unlike Doris, was quite bright) everything is relative. And that means that the amount of exercise that I do, relative to the fact that I rarely otherwise move, is therefore far greater than the amount of exercise that Doris does, given that she normally moves a lot, especially when she's at work.

It's a bit like that story in the bible, where Jesus says that the poor woman who just gave a farthing to the temple treasury actually gave more than the millionaire bloke, because she gave everything she had.

I forget the exact monetary figures involved, but that was the gist of it. And, even though I'm sure that the temple accountant was glad that there was a rich bloke in the mix somewhere, nevertheless you can see the point Jesus was trying to make.

It's basically the same thing as Einstein's theory, which just proves that Jesus was way ahead of his time.

You see, to someone like me, who spends most of the day either in bed or on the sofa, a quick stroll to the kitchen is massive. It's the equivalent of Doris, who's normally on her feet all day at work, running a marathon.

So, in effect, as Doris doesn't run marathons, I'm doing more exercise than she is. And remember, that's not just my opinion, it's the opinion of both Einstein and Jesus.

Anyway, I could tell that I was going to have real trouble convincing Doris that I'm right, and that I should cut down on exercise, so I asked her to get me a book from the library on Einstein's Theory of Relativity (I didn't tell her why) so I can secretly gen up on all the facts.

Obviously, I could have walked to the library myself to get the book, but that would have involved exercise and defeated the object.

Doris says she will get me the book tonight. Little does she know that I will then use it to prove my point about exercise scientifically, beyond any reasonable doubt, and then humiliate her mercilessly with my superior intellect.

I will report back.

13th March

This Einstein book is fascinating.

However, as bright was he obviously was, I think I've spotted some flaws in his theory. Bear with me, because this stuff is a bit complicated, but well worth getting your head around if you can.

To be honest, I didn't really expect to be getting into the whole business of totally disproving Einstein's space/time continuum in this diary, but needs must. Pride is at stake. And no doubt the scientific community will thank me for it one day, even if it means them having to reprint all their journals and encyclopedias, which I imagine might cost them a few quid.

I'll take it from the top.

Albert Einstein - you may have heard of him - argued that the traditional Newtonian idea of absolute time should be superseded by a different notion of time, where time was the fourth dimension in a space-time continuum.

Now, I know what you're all thinking. What the fuck does that mean?

Well, yes, by all means please do stop me if I'm going too fast for you, because I know there's a few Brummies out there.

In other words, what Einstein meant was that time itself is

not just something totally separate that just ticks along like clockwork in the background, regardless of what else is going on. Time itself is actually always changing, relative to where you are in space, and how fast you're moving.

Still confused? Right. Concentrate for a minute – here's the nub of it.

Einstein said that the laws of physics are the same for all **non**-accelerating observers, but the moment somebody starts to move, through space, then relative to that, time actually starts to move slower.

So, in a nutshell, what he's saying is, the faster you move, the slower time goes. And this, Einstein says, gets more and more noticeable as you travel faster and faster, until eventually, you reach the speed of light (186,000 miles a second) at which point, time would, theoretically, stop altogether.

I say theoretically, because it's never been possible to test this, because we can't make anything travel at the speed of light – except of course, light itself, and a few politicians running away from the electorate.

Right, I can sense that a few of you are still looking a bit puzzled, so let's look at a real-life example.

According to Albert Einstein, if an astronaut went up into space, and was whizzing around at thousands of miles an hour on his special mission for let's say... a year, he will actually be ageing slower than the people on earth. So while it's been a year for him, it could actually mean that ten years have passed on earth in that same period.

Got it? So, the astronaut buggers off, for what, according

to his watch, is a year. He then comes back to earth, and discovers his twin brother is now ten years older than him.

Well, nice try, Mr Einstein. But I'm not buying it. Because we all know that the exact opposite is true, and that time actually goes much slower when you don't move at all.

It's called boredom. Try spending three hours on the M5 motorway going down to Weston-Super-Mare, and you'll soon see what I mean.

Let's do a scientific experiment.

Two identical cars, two identical passengers.

One car is going at a constant seventy miles an hour, all the way down to Weston.

The other car is stuck at Sandwell viaduct, not moving at all, for three fucking hours.

Now you tell me, for which passenger, in which car, has time passed the slowest?

And I should know, because exactly that happened to me. And, Einstein or no Einstein, that's three hours of my life I'm never going to get back.

Now Albert, of course, was basically a good bloke, who just bit off more than he could chew. But you have to admire his efforts. And remember, he had to work without the aid of any modern computers. And crucially, the M5 and Sandwell viaduct didn't exist when he was around, so unlike me, he had no way to properly measure his theories.

Luckily, I was able to pick up his work where he left off, and sort things out for him.

The fact remains though, he's still right about exercise all being relative to how much you move. So I still maintain that I do far more exercise that Doris.

It's not what she wants to hear, but you can't ignore the laws of physics.

15th March

Nightmare scenario.

Doris has developed a slight tickle in the throat, so she's sent off for three home testing kits for Covid – one for her, one for me, and one for Jack.

I've told her, there's no way I'm poking anything down my throat again – not after the incident with the DJ when I was 18 – but she's insisting. She says she won't come to my house again until I test negative, which practically makes her Hitler. Well, it does in my book, and this is my book.

How ironic, this being the fifteenth of March – the Ides of March. That's when Brutus stabbed Caesar in the back. And now Doris has done the same to me.

Anyway, for those that don't know, the testing kit consists of a small stick with a swab on the end. They ask you to rub it over both tonsils, without touching your tongue, and then you have to ram it up your nose and wiggle it about. This, they say in the instructions, 'might make you feel a little uncomfortable.'

I told Doris I'd rather shove a hedgehog up my arse, but she said that's not going to help either of us, and it's certainly not going to help the hedgehog.

Anyway, after a long, difficult negotiation I said I'd give it a go, but I'm not promising anything.

I'll report back.

16th March

The home testing kit was designed by Frankenstein.

For a start off, you need set aside about three months to read the instructions, and have a PhD just to understand them. Secondly, there's no way I can put a stick down my throat without gagging.

It says you're not supposed to touch your tongue, but that's impossible unless you dislocate your jaw.

The moment the swab stick hit the back of my tongue I projectile-vomited and spat it straight into the kitchen sink. Exactly the same as happened before with that DJ. And to compound matters, the sink was full of soapy water and bleach, so I doubt even NCIS could get a result from that.

I told Doris to forget it, but she's like a Rottweiler lately, so she's sent for another kit and says she'll do it for me – perhaps when I'm asleep.

I'll report back.

17th March

I woke up in the armchair to find Doris trying to ram a stick down my throat. I gagged so badly I head-butted her. It's possible that I broke her nose. But she wouldn't give up. To be fair, she'd come prepared.

She was wearing full PPE - hard hat, gloves, mask and boots - and she'd Gaffa-taped a mirror and a torch onto a broom handle, in a desperate attempt to see my tonsils. "Good luck with that," I said, "I had the buggers taken out when I was eleven."

Undaunted, she re-read the instructions, which stated that if you have no tonsils you have to swab where they used to be. Sadly, that still meant the back of the throat, so she had one final desperate stab at it, this time using the spare Gaffa tape to restrain my arms and head.

"That'll have to do" she said, ripping the chewed-up stick from my gritted teeth. "Now I just have to ram it up your nose and wiggle it about."

You don't want to know my response, but it wasn't kindly.

"You'll thank me for this one day," she added.

At this point I kicked her very hard on both shins, just to remind her that today wasn't going to be that day.

18th March

What a bloody farce.

Having gone through all the rigmarole of home testing, then comes the Laurel and Hardy moment. Apparently, the same day that Doris sent for the Covid tests, Jack had his NHS bowel cancer testing kit come through the post.

Suffice it to say, various bits and pieces were left on the kitchen table for a few days, and communication became blurred. Doris meekly admitted to me afterwards that there was a "slight chance" that Jack may have got some of the samples mixed up when he posted them off.

The consequences don't bear thinking about. It's possible that the lab technician may think that Jack's arse has got a new variant of Covid. Or, even worse still, that one of his bowel samples was found up my nose.

Let's just hope that there wasn't a cock-up. Otherwise the next 24 hours could be interesting.

Whatever happens, this mustn't spoil my plans. It's World Sleep Day tomorrow, and I intend to celebrate in style.

19th March

Just woke up to a phone call from the NHS.

They're sending a helicopter to get me. The woman on the other end kept telling me to stay calm. I was calm.

I told Doris to call the NHS. This is her mess, she can get me out of it.

On the plus side though, I was thinking of treating myself to a helicopter ride for my birthday, so this might save me a hundred quid.

20th March

What a stupid day yesterday was.

After about five hours on the phone, followed by a quick impromptu press conference, Doris finally sorted out the confusion.

I did get my helicopter ride, but I had to share it with two blokes in full Chernobyl-style nuclear fall-out protective suits – the sort of thing they wore when all the scientists came to get ET. And, of course, they made me wear one as well. They certainly weren't taking any chances with this new strain of Arse Covid. When we landed, three minutes later, half the world's press were waiting for me.

When Doris had explained everything, they quickly lost interest in me, and the hospital said I had to get the bus back. Bollocks to that. I made Doris phone Jack to come and pick me up in the car.

I kept the nuclear-waste protective suit, though. It might come in handy if I ever have to do my own shopping. Cloth face masks make me feel a bit claustrophobic, but the full headgear gives you a bit more breathing space. There'd be room to smoke a pipe in there. Or even vape, if you were that way inclined.

Actually, I reckon all smokers should be made to wear them, for the sake of the rest of us. There could perhaps be a little exhaust pipe at the back so they didn't totally die, but otherwise it'd clean up the environment nicely.

It would also put paid to the notion that smoking makes you look cool, because wearing a full bio-hazard suit in a pub or nightclub isn't usually a great look.

21st March

Doris's cough seems better now.

But she won't let the topic drop – the woman's become obsessed. She's now insisting that we both have the jab, and she's even booked me in online at Bilston Methodist Church to have one of the Vauxhall Astra vaccines.

I'm in two minds, both of which say no.

But Doris has once again threatened to withdraw her labour if I refuse. I reckon this could end up going to the European Court of Human Rights, or whatever the new equivalent is when you've left Europe. Judge Judy off the telly, probably. Or that gay one with the unusual name - Judge Grinder, I think it is. They'd sort this out in seconds.

Bottom line, Doris isn't allowed to control my body. And refusing to clean or cook for me is discrimination. After all, my money's as good as anybody else's, even though I don't technically give her any of it.

22nd March

More chaos.

I've just texted Doris to say I'm not happy about having the jab. And before you say anything, it's got nothing to do with my irrational fear of needles, or my general cowardice, or the conspiracy theories. It's because I heard on the BBC news (so it must be true) that some countries were suspending the Vauxhall Astra vaccine because it's been linked with the formation of large clots.

But of course, nothing in life is straightforward, and I only discovered later that my phone's autocorrect spell-checker thingy had decided to change clots to clits. Next thing I knew, Doris was ringing me in a major panic. In fact I've never heard her quite so rattled.

There's no way she's having a larger clit, she ranted. She's quite happy with the one she's got, and if necessary she'd rather wear a mask for the rest of her life, so they can take their vaccine and stick it up their arse.

I think the whole clit thing had hit rather a tender spot with Doris, if I'm honest. I didn't want to pry, but I suspect it's because her's has always been just small enough to ensure that Jack can never find it, and that's the way she likes it.

Doris has never been that way inclined, you see – never much of a one for that rumpy pumpy stuff. Hence, no kids. She's a bit like me in that respect, except I've got three kids, but that's not really any of my doing. I was just a passive onlooker.

The first kid was an accident, and the other two were a disaster and a catastrophe, in that order.

Three kids, in two and a half years, by four different fathers, and not one of them stuck around long enough to even flush the chain.

Anyway, that's another story, and if you want the rest of it you'll have to buy my autobiography. But for now, thanks to the accidental clot-clit autocorrect, it was a good result for me. Doris cancelled our vaccine appointments.

No doubt she'll find out the truth about the clots in due course when she eventually finds time to watch the news, but I reckon she'll be too embarrassed to ever bring up the topic again.

Job done.

23rd March

It's the anniversary of Lockdown. One year ago today.

To celebrate, I did fuck all.

Also, as a gesture of goodwill, I let Doris have the day off, and I didn't try to humiliate her about her lack of exercise, or threaten to take her to court. That woman's very lucky to have me as a neighbour.

Others wouldn't so thoughtful.

24th March

The weather was quite mild today.

Small hints of spring. So I wandered out into the garden. It's funny - lockdown has given me time to notice things I never noticed before.

For instance, I have a garden pond at home. Yes, I had noticed that before, but never really studied it. It's not very big - in fact it's about the size of a fish - but it now hosts a fascinating, self-sustaining mini eco-system.

There's plants, insects, those waterboatman things, the odd newt (or is it a tadpole? I never knew the difference) a couple of frogs, and a bloated toad who I named George (after my favourite billionaire, George Soros) all living quite happily together. And of course, a small fish. In fact, several small fish.

It all started when I won two goldfish at a fairground many years ago (well, I say won, you just had to give the bloke a quid and miss with a hoop and you got a fish, so I had two goes and missed twice).

Anyway, not happy with the idea of them living in a plastic bag, I popped the fish in the pond and left them to it.

Now, many years and several generations later, they seem to have made a nice home for themselves.

There's about sixteen of them these days - orange, black, and some sort of in-between.

They've somehow become multicultural. In fact, they'd be ideal goldfish for a TV advert, so if any ad agencies are interested, email me and I'll rent them out.

Anyway, I think that's pretty impressive. I've never fed them, so they've obviously learnt to live off the land, so to speak, and adapt to their surroundings naturally.

In fact, they've been in there so long, it wouldn't surprise me if one or two of them have ventured out onto the land and evolved into monkeys.

On that subject – just a quick aside.

It's not just Einstein's work that I've trashed over the years - I also once disproved Darwin's theory of evolution. And it only took me a couple of hours one afternoon.

Let me say from the start, that I don't blame Darwin. Like Einstein, he was a good bloke doing his best.

But his theory of evolution, frankly, is bollocks.

Yes, Darwin lived in more primitive times. But from the moment it was first uttered, his theory should have rung alarm bells, because it does pose some very troublesome questions – questions that I'm amazed nobody has ever raised before.

For instance:

Question One: If we're all evolved from monkeys, how come we've still got some monkeys?

Were these just the lazy monkeys? The monkeys that just couldn't be arsed to evolve?

Did somebody, millions of years ago, send some of the monkeys to Grammar School, and then just tell the rest that they had to go and work up a tree? If so, who was it? Was it a bloke, or was it a monkey? If it was a bloke, where did he come from, and if it was a monkey, how did he learn to talk? It doesn't make sense.

Question Two: If, as Darwin insisted, monkeys evolved from fish, how come monkeys can't swim?

And if monkeys can swim, (because I haven't bothered to check) how come I can't? Surely if I'd have evolved from a fish, I'd be able to swim at least a width.

Clearly, Darwin hadn't thought this through. So a few summers back I decided to investigate myself by visiting Dudley Zoo.

There was no evidence, as far as I could see, that any of the monkeys there could have evolved from fish. Apart from anything else, the fish were kept in a separate tank, several metres away, making interbreeding impossible. And the monkeys themselves were locked up behind glass. The ultimate contraception.

But I know what you're thinking – what about monkeys in the wild?

Well, I'm nothing if not thorough in my research, so in

order to experience monkeys in the wild I went to the West Midlands Safari Park, only to discover that they hadn't got any monkeys any more.

Bastards.

But however you look at this, we always come back to the fundamental question. What would make one fish want to become a monkey, and another fish think: 'No, I'm all right as I am, thanks. I'll stop as a fish.' Is it just a love of swimming versus a love of trees?

If so, there must have been a point, somewhere in history, when a fish who wanted to be a monkey tried to climb a tree. It would, of course, have died about halfway up, thus ending his chance to breed with other dead fish littering the floor who also wanted to be monkeys.

In short, they had no chance. Survival of the fittest? Not if you're dead. Think again, Mr Darwin.

Anyway – where was I? Oh yes. My fish pond.

I've watched a lot of protests and street riots in London on the news – especially during lockdown. And it's made me realise something. I think it's always better to be a big fish in a small pond. And it's even more vital if you're a small fish. It's your pond. You own a piece of it. You care about it. You can influence it. You can help protect it and improve it, and you're more likely to want to.

But most importantly of all, in your pond, YOU matter. You, your opinions, your ideas and your dreams won't get swallowed up by the bigger fish.

So no, I've never fed my fish.

They quickly learnt to stand on their own two fins. As far as I'm aware they've never even had any EU funding. They feed themselves.

As the old saying goes: 'Give a fish some food, and it eats for a day. But teach a fish how to fish…'

That's as much as I can remember.

25th March

Some sad news.

Ethel Grainger – third door down opposite – has passed away suddenly. And what's more, it was Covid-related.

Well, sort of.

Apparently, she was in her dressing gown putting out the recycling last Tuesday morning, when an ambulance carrying a suspected Covid patient whizzed past her, all sirens blaring. That wouldn't have alerted Ethel, though, who's as deaf as a post, and who was standing quite close to the kerb trying to stamp on some soggy cardboard that had blown away in the night.

Sadly, according to the eye witness, she lost her footing at the wrong time, and the ambulance's wing mirror clipped her on the side of the jaw at around 40 mph. I'm guessing that this was no picnic for a frail old lady. Anyway, she landed upside down in the green bin.

"Had it not been for the serious nature of the virus, the ambulance driver wouldn't have been in such a rush," the coroner concluded. "So I'm afraid it has to go down as a Covid-related death."

The irony is, Tuesday wasn't even Ethel's recycling day, so it was all avoidable.

Luckily, I hear that the suspected Covid patient is now fully-recovered, so at least he won't go down as another Covid-related death, unless he dies for some reason.

So I suppose it all evens out in the end.

I've always thought it a very strange rule that ambulances aren't allowed to treat any people that they've run over themselves – especially given that they're likely to be first on the scene. I guess it's considered tampering with the evidence. But anyway, I doubt that would have helped Ethel, who was quite brittle at the best of times.

It's a sobering testament to the force of the trauma that her dentures were later discovered in the Royal Mail postbox, over fifty yards away.

26th March

Doris says it's Ethel's funeral next week. Cremation.

Personally, I think they should have just left her in the green bin. I don't mean that in a harsh way. I've spoken to Ethel a few times over the years, and she was always very passionate about green issues and recycling.

I think it's what Ethel would have wanted, even though her daughter doesn't agree with me. A simple ceremony, and then turn her into compost for hanging baskets, or bone meal for rescue dogs or something.

Besides, cremations can't be good for global warming.

27th March

Today, apparently, is World Theatre Day. I'm sure they'll be thrilled as they're all shut.

In an idle moment (it does happen) I looked into the other 'World Something Days', because we seem to get a lot of them lately. It turns out there's over a hundred, in fact.

Here's some that caught my eye:

21st February celebrates 'International Mother Language Day'. I'm sure my mother would have liked that – her language was vile.

20th March is 'International Day of Happiness'. Fuck that.

17th June is 'World Day to Combat Desertification and Drought' – but I expect you already knew that.

On 30th June we have 'International Asteroid Day', lest we should ever forget asteroids.

28th September is 'World Rabies Day' – our chance to all gather round and celebrate rabies.

2nd October is 'International Day of Non-Violence' – so presumably it's okay to be violent throughout the rest of the year.

There's also a 'World Teachers' Day' (must have been quite tricky to find a day when they weren't all on holiday), an 'International Anti-Corruption Day' (I can guarantee that somebody's making a fortune out of that) and even a 'World Soil Day' which, in case you want to nip out and buy a card to send off to your favourite bit of soil, is the 5th October.

Pop it in your diary. I have.

28th March

I'm told by Doris that the clocks went forward in the night, and consequently I lost an hour's sleep. So I'm now going to spend the rest of the day trying to find it.

29th March

Another milestone announcement from Boris.

From today, I'm legally allowed to see Doris outside. That may sound like progress, but to be honest, she's not much use to me outside, except for occasionally cutting the lawn.

Most of the work here is inside – cooking, cleaning, washing up, and so on – and she's still allowed to do that illegally – so I don't think the new rules will make that much difference to us.

One other thing I did notice in the announcement is that weddings are now happening again, but only for up to six people. Not that we had any lockdown restrictions in my youth, but that would just about have been enough to accommodate my wedding – me, the bloke, the vicar and the three kids – six in total.

As luck would have it, he didn't bother turning up, and neither did I, so we'd have had room to spare.

Actually, that reminds me – I must ask the kids sometime how that day went.

They probably loved it. More sausage rolls and cake for them.

1st April

April Fool's Day again. I say again, because it was April Fool's Day last year as well. Well, it is every year, but what I mean is, last year on April Fool's Day I remember we were still in lockdown, and here we are again, so nothing's really changed. Just a whole year gone.

No doubt the news programmes will all be rolling out their pathetic spoof April Fool's stories. Some of them used to be quite good, in the days before they all started panicking about being irresponsible, or offending people.

In 2010, a local newspaper from Jordan called Al Ghad announced that a UFO had landed in the region. It caused mass panic and chaos.

The town's mayor, a bloke by the name of Mohammed Mleihan, was fooled by the prank, and sent off his security guards in search of the aliens.

They even then started evacuating all of the town's 13,000 residents, who were by this time screaming hysterically and fearing for their lives.

The newspaper later apologised for the joke, which is a shame. Because I think that's quite funny.

But of course these days it's a different story. Newspapers and TV now have to desperately search for something that isn't racist, or sexist, or ageist, or idiotist, or some other sort of 'ist.' And that's virtually impossible.

So now we usually end up with some lame bollocks from a grinning, cheesy newsreader telling an unconvincing story about a rabbit that has learnt to play the piano in his spare time or something, in the vain hope that no-one on the planet can possibly take offence.

But of course they can, and do.

Because even lame stories about rabbits playing pianos are rabbitist. And, I suppose, pianist.

2nd April

Easter bank holiday today.

Bank holidays are a great British institution. This one's very different, of course, being in lockdown, but usually they follow a pattern. I particularly like the August bank holidays.

For a start, it normally rains - not just cats and dogs, but a whole menagerie, including locusts and frogs in biblical proportions.

Despite this, huge swathes of the local population gather their buckets and spades and take part in the ancient pagan festival of lining up to park on the M5.

The M5, of course, is the gateway to Poldark Land, unlike its sister motorway the M6, which I can confirm doesn't actually go anywhere.

For the less ambitious, the M5 is also handy for seaside bank holiday stop-offs like Weston-Super-Mare.

As I recently mentioned in my diary (whilst disproving Einstein) I myself recently undertook the spiritual journey to Weston to do a live show, and spent many, many happy hours staring at the brake lights of the lorry in front, and trying to decide which receptacle in the car I would eventually have to wee in.

In the end I opted for the Starbucks coffee cup, on the basis that it probably wouldn't affect the taste.

At one point I'd passed a huge sign on the side of the road with a Facebook logo on it. 'Follow us on Facebook!' it said, adding a jaunty exclamation mark to make it sound really fun. As it happened, I was desperate for some fun, and also for some bladder distraction, so I reached for my phone (I wasn't driving, but then again neither was the driver) and glanced up at the sign to see which dynamic entertaining business name I should type into the search box and engage with.

It turned out to be Sandwell Viaduct.

Really? Has social media really sunk to this? Who the hell follows a viaduct on Facebook? How desperate have you got to be to actually 'like' the page of a fucking viaduct?

For that matter, what is a viaduct? And do I need one in my life? Only if I can wee in one, I decided – but I think that's an aqueduct.

I did eventually get to Weston, but the journey took so long that I had to shave my legs twice on the way.

Nobody does roadworks quite like the British on a bank holiday. '288 people are employed on this project' said the signage. That's 287 invisible people employed putting out the signage, and one man looking into a hole.

And those who don't boldly seek out Poldark Land, or the Poundshop Poldark Land of Weston, inevitably aim their Sat-Navs at Wales.

I'm told by scientists that there are some days when it's not actually raining in Wales, but I think they're lying. Probably just another part of the climate change scam.

Some strange folk even make the long trek to Wales in order just to sit in a large tin box – presumably because it's more comfortable than their house, and it makes the rain sound louder.

Others, even more strange, take the tin box with them, attached to the back of their car, like some kind of tourist hermit crab. Or perhaps a better analogy would be a tourist snail, given the speed they're driving.

Not content with the rain at home, these fanatics seek out remote sodden peat bog fields where they can settle down and experience some proper, more consistent Welsh rain. They listen to it beating out a tribal rhythm on the tin roof while desperately leafing through pamphlets that look as though they were printed in 1950, advertising fun days for the whole family at exotic destinations like Barometer World, Paperweight World, Sheep World, Lamb World, Goat World, Wasp World, Wood Louse World or, for the real hard-core thrill seekers and adrenaline junkies, Stick Insect World, where many of the exhibits are actually sticks.

But caravans, traffic jams, crap weather and dodgy tourist attractions isn't the worst of it. There's something else about the August bank holiday which is even more depressing. The fact that it seems to give a green light to certain businesses that's it's now okay to start talking about Christmas.

Yes, the first 'Now Booking for Xmas' signs have already started to appear at venues. Whenever I see one I have to resist a strong urge to put a brick through their window, with a bit of tinsel sellotaped to it, and a polite note saying 'Too Early'.

3rd April

Found myself getting a bit bored lately, so Doris has offered to pop round with some books for me.

I do love reading actually, despite having a very bad start in life. After all, I went to Tipton School, so I had no formal education.

And it's been a tough journey for me.

My school experience was like a roller coaster, without the ups, and along the way I was constantly blighted by rare afflictions, such as Lazy Cow Syndrome, and the lesser-known HDAD, which is dyslexic bad behaviour in High Definition.

In those days, of course, dyslexia wasn't even a condition, it was just another word we didn't know how to spell. And I was diagnosed quite late in life, because apparently it's much harder for them to tell if you've got dyslexia if you can't read.

It turned out, after further exhaustive testing, that I'm only dyslexic in one eye. Nevertheless it was a very confusing time. And it wasn't helped by the fact that they discovered that I'm colour blind.

I had absolutely no idea, so as you can imagine, this came

as a real bolt from the orange. They only first suspected the condition when the doctor visited my house and saw the wallpaper and curtains, which I thought matched. That probably also explains, actually, why I turned up to my Aunty Miriam's funeral wearing lime green.

As a young girl I grew up within spitting distance, quite literally, of a fine old institution called The Cock Inn. I was the only child of a pub landlady, which meant that, for a full eighteen years, I wasn't even old enough to go into my own lounge.

So I spent hour after hour, listening to the distant prattle of drunken men below, while I was locked in a tiny, cold, magnolia room, lit by a single dingy light bulb dangling from a ceiling rose which swung gently in the draught from the broken window.

Reading, therefore, became my solace.

And I read anything that came to hand. Beer mats, the old scraps of newspapers which formed my carpet's underlay, and, most usefully of all, the graffiti on the pub toilet walls.

This graffiti, in my early formative years, acted as my English teacher, and helped me to develop a love of fine words – especially ones with four-letters – and also, of poetry.

All of this, of course, was both fascinating and educational to an inquisitive two year old.

So, as soon as I was old enough to venture out alone, at about two and a half, I secretly visited the nearest library, in Tipton, only to discover it was shut.

The stories of A.A. Milne, in particular, had a profound effect on my life. The day I discovered the true origins of Piglet, for example, I became a vegetarian. The only time I ever break this rule is if I decide to have a bacon sarnie or some scratchings, and that's only if I'm very hungry.

And I also learnt the power of positive thinking from this one small extract, taken from 'Winnie the Pooh and the Blustery Day.'

A worried looking piglet says:

> "Supposing a tree fell down, Pooh, when we were underneath it?"
> "Supposing it didn't," said Pooh, after careful thought.
> Piglet was comforted by this.

I will forever be grateful to Winnie the Pooh, for giving me back my early childhood.

Anyway, as I say – Doris is going to bring me some books round soon. Not sure if her tastes in reading will match mine. She's probably a bit more into crime drama than Winnie The Pooh, but we'll see.

It'll be good to be inspired once again by fine literature.

4th April

Fucking hell.

I've just received a pile of Barbara Cartland books.

I didn't expect Doris would be exactly Stephen Fry in her pursuit of the fine arts, but I thought she might at least rise up above Barbara Cartland.

Don't get me wrong. Barbara was a very important literary figure, because she was, by any literary measure, the one who wrote the most books.

I did a bit of research on her. Let's just have a quick look at some of her remarkable statistics.

By the time she died in the year 2000, she'd managed to publish (get ready for this) 723 novels. At her peak in 1983, Barbara was averaging one book every two weeks. Remember, that's writing them, not just reading them, and it's a feat which then put her into another famous book - The Guinness Book of Records.

She was also, by far, the pinkest of all the novelists. No other novelist, before or since, has ever been that pink.

Barbara, in case you didn't know, was also a local wench. Yep, she was born in Birmingham, and she was related to the Royal Family. In fact, Diana, Princess of Wales, was her step-granddaughter.

Barbara's lack of writing prowess didn't seem to damage her bank balance though. In total, she sold 750 million copies of her books. Yes, 750 million. But with your help, I'm hoping to beat that record, so I've had 800 million copies of this diary printed.

There's no doubt, Barbara was a remarkable woman. And even after she died, she didn't really stop. Not content with actually publishing 723 novels, they then discovered, in her loft, another 160 novels that she hadn't yet got around to publishing. Lazy Cow.

By the way, you might think I'm making these numbers up for comic effect, but I'm not. You can check them in Wankepedia.

So that's 883 books in total. And I'm going to show you a

short extract from just one them…

"I love you, my darling!" he said.

"I love you so overwhelmingly, so completely, that it is going to take me a lifetime to tell you how much you mean to me."

"I love you…too!" Alexia murmured. "But there do not seem to be enough words in which to…express it."

"I told you your vocabulary was limited," the Marquis said with a smile.

Christ.

That's one paragraph, from one chapter. Can you imagine reading a whole book of that, and then saying to yourself, "I quite enjoyed that novel, so I think I'll just nip out to WHSmith and buy the other 882, at an approximate cost of thirteen thousand quid."

No. You'd chuck yourself off a bloody cliff first wouldn't you? I mean – listen to this:

"She felt a sudden flame shoot through her body; she felt as if he drew her like a magnet into his keeping and that he would never let her go. She felt her lips respond to his and knew that this was a love which would never alter or grow less.

She felt him draw her closer still… until they were one; indivisible - one heart, one soul, one love for all eternity."

I especially like that last bit: "She felt him draw her closer still…until they were one."

I think that's just a posh way of saying they had a shag.

Anyway, I won't be reading the Barbara Cartland novels, so I've instructed Doris to come and collect them. All 883 of them.

She's ordered a skip.

5th April

The books have gone, but the boredom remains.

I desperately need a new hobby. Doris suggested buying a dog, but I think I can rule that out on the grounds of not liking dogs, and the fact that dogs generally tend to need walking on a daily basis. And that's the last thing Doris needs – she's busy enough. Anyway, I will do some more research and report back.

6th April

I've done some research, and I think I might try and learn how to play the saxophone. It shouldn't be too tricky, because I haven't got one.

From what I can see online, most people only have a problem learning how to play a saxophone when they actually start to blow into one. Up until then it's relatively plain sailing. I'm torn. I do like the saxophone. But then again, I might start to hate the saxophone if I try to learn how to play one and it doesn't go quite as well as I imagined. It's a terrible trait, but I know what I'm like. Very impatient, just like my mother. In fact, come to think of it, she couldn't play the saxophone either.

But I just know that if I do buy one and I'm not playing the solo from Baker Street in less than ten minutes, I'll lose interest and smash it up the wall, just like I did with the triangle last year. So, on balance, I've ruled it out. Along with growing my own tomatoes, ballroom dancing, getting fit, buying a dog, learning another language, anger management classes, and being nice to people.

7th April

Bizarre weather over this bank holiday week.

Just two days ago it was lovely, warm and sunny. Today it snows.

The scientists and green mob will no doubt quickly blame it on climate change, and stick a few million quid on our taxes. Not that I pay taxes, but I do occasionally feel sorry for those that do.

No-one can seriously argue that the climate isn't changing. It tends to do that. Has done since the beginning of time. Even the dinosaurs noticed it, and then took immediate evasive action by dying.

However, the science is complicated and, a bit like Brexit, it tends to sharply divide opinion.

I, of course, am no expert on climate change - at least not yet. But I have decided that I'd like to look into this topic, to discover what's really going on, and then try to explain it to you in language that we can all understand, unless you're a Brummie.

So that's it then – that's my next major project to stave off the boredom of lockdown. Something I can really get my teeth into.

After all, I recently sorted Einstein's Theory of Relativity and Darwin's Theory of Evolution, so climate change should be a piece of piss.

I'll borrow Doris's computer for research, and report back in a couple of days.

9th April

My research into climate change has been interrupted by some sad news.

It's today been announced that Prince Philip – the Queen's bloke – has passed away, aged 99.

Anyone who's read my autobiology will know that I'm a huge fan of HMV The Queen. She's been a fantastic role model to me all these years, proving that it's possible to bring up a dysfunctional family while living off benefits.

Prince Philip was her rock and companion for 68 years – stylish, dignified, brave, and always delightfully non-PC, which is the way I like my Royals. He was never afraid to tease foreigners, on or off the battlefield, and he also had an acerbic wit that some delicate creatures would consider 'inappropriate' – which is always a good sign that he's on to something.

Yes, I know that there are now many people out there that consider the monarchy to be an out-dated institution, and to them I say: 'Well, of course it is, that's the whole point. The monarchy is meant to be crusty, weird, and totally out of touch with us ordinary folks – they're Royal. They need to be different.'

Their ancestry stretches directly back to Henry the Eighth and beyond, so what exactly do you expect the monarchy to be? Some sort of trendy online virtual experience with its own Facebook page and an App? Perhaps you'd prefer a small clique of vegan, super-woke, ridiculously-entitled, brand-conscious tossers with their own YouTube channel entitled: 'The Only Way is Windsor?' If so, Meghan's the future.

Or, more likely, you'd prefer nothing at all. Just a grey world where we're all the same. Not for me.

Anyway, I liked Philip, even though I never met him. The world needs characters, and despite all his later privileges he had a tough start in life. RIP Philip. Such a shame he had to clock out today. Just a few months more, and he would have received a telegram from his wife.

10th April

Right then – climate change.

Here's what I've found out so far. Though I say it myself, this is a major piece of work, worthy of a knighthood. Or perhaps a night hood. One day, the scientific community will call me Dame Doreen, the Climate Change Queen.

It took me ages to research this, and even longer for Doris to type it all up. So settle back, stick on your patio heater, and I'll explain.

Climate Change is the new name for 'Global Warming'. It was quickly re-branded after a few inconvenient graphs stubbornly refused to show any real evidence of warming whatsoever for the past 20 years.

Now, at this point, I imagine lots of you on one side of the debate will be jumping up and down and swearing at me, pointing furiously at pictures of baby polar bears clinging helplessly to a melting iceberg, and calling for me to be burnt at the stake. Others, of course, will point to the fact that burning someone at the stake is not good for your carbon footprint.

And that's the first major problem with the climate change science. The real experts themselves can't always agree.

Greta Thunberg, for example, was recently criticised by another leading climate change expert, Meat Loaf. He said that she'd been brainwashed by those around her. Greta's parents are currently working on her response.

Miss Thunberg, by the way, before anybody gets on their hobby horse, is now the wrong side of eighteen, so the usual defence of her being a child and therefore beyond any critical analysis, has given way to the ravages of time.

Anyway, the range of opinions on this topic is interesting. Some say that we're doomed if we don't instantly stop breathing, because all human beings are total bastards.

Others are a bit more optimistic, and say we'll be all right if we all ditch our gas-guzzling cars, and spend the rest of our lives standing at bus stops.

Electric vehicles, of course, according to the TV adverts, will definitely help save the planet. That's unless we have to charge them up, because then it involves electricity.

Electricity, unlike apples, doesn't grow on trees.

Some of it comes from cuddly green renewable sources, like solar, wind and waves. But that's only about enough to charge up your mobile phone and Alexa. All the rest has to come from nuclear or coal-fired power plants.

In an effort to solve this dilemma, some 'gas stations' in America have now introduced electric car charging points, powered by…yes, diesel generators. You couldn't make it up, could you?

So, if you absolutely have to travel - for instance, to get to the pub or the benefits office – by far the greenest way to do it is to buy an electric car to show off to the neighbours, park it permanently on your drive, and then walk.

Or, of course, if you live near a canal, like me, you could travel by canoe. At least as far as the nearest lock. And if you don't happen to live by water, don't worry, because you soon will do, thanks to the floods.

But bear in mind that most canoes these days are made of plastic, and plastic is basically the new Hitler.

Therefore your new plastic canoe could, if not disposed of properly, get tangled up with penguins, shopping trolleys, Sir David Attenborough, and other wildlife. So if you do buy a canoe to save the planet, make sure you leave it at home.

Other scientists, however, reckon that climate change is nothing to do with transport. It's all down to cows farting. The latest research shows that one single cow fart can increase the air temperature by up to seven degrees – especially if you're trapped in a lift with it.

Luckily, cows tend not to use lifts too often, but it can happen, so check first. And of course, cow farts are still a danger to polar bears who, even from the other side of the world, have a very keen sense of smell.

To stop this potential disaster, some claim that we all need to become vegans. But there is a problem with their logic. Because even if I start eating nothing but lentils, a cow can still fart. Whereas, if I kill it and eat it, it can't.

And surely the even bigger question here is, whether a life

spent eating lentils and Linda McCartney sausages is a life worth saving?

Others believe that wind isn't the problem – it's the solution.

Wind farms are now all the rage. Trouble is, it isn't always windy (just on bank holidays) so they're inefficient and often grind to a halt. That's a problem if you're halfway though charging your electric canoe.

But once again, the scientists seem to have overlooked the obvious solution. Get the cows to fart on the turbines to make them spin – job done.

We all like to do our bit, of course. I myself went carbon neutral in 2020. I have an extension lead which runs into Doris's house, and now get all my electricity from her.

Meanwhile, the EU's solution to the climate change crisis was brilliant in its simplicity. They passed laws making all the hairdryers and all the vacuum cleaners half-power.

So now we all have to spend twice as long drying our hair and hoovering, which puts a major strain on the national grid. But that's all fine by the EU. Because our electricity companies are now owned by France and Germany.

Some scientists, however, say that - whatever we do - we're still doomed. Why? Because, they argue, the sun's solar activity is what controls our climate, and CO_2 levels have been rising for the past 10,000 years, and there's bugger all we can do about it.

So, is this problem bigger than all of us? We all remember the story of King Canute, who thought he could stop the tide coming in. By the way, King Canute - that's a modern spelling of his name. That's the English spelling they used in school books. His actual original Danish name - and this is true - was King Cnut. Make of that what you will...I reckon it's an anagram.

But anyway, whether it's King Canute or a total Cnut, the question still remains - can mere mortals like us really push back the rising sea levels, or alter the entire planet's behaviour?

Well, one American scientist recently calculated that if we spend 1,000 trillion tax dollars on climate change projects over the next 100 years we might, just might, impact the earth's temperature by 0.01 %.

About as noticeable as a cow fart in a hurricane.

And in the meantime, of course, a few folk who have their fingers in green pies would be getting extraordinarily rich.

Never mind the oil and tobacco companies – green is now the world's biggest business, especially if you can get the right scare messages out there.

So what's the truth of it? Is climate change the world's biggest crisis? Or the world's greatest scam? Only time will tell.

Most scientists do agree on one thing though. To solve the problem, it will need lots more funding...for scientists.

I was recently reminded by an old Facebook post that when we were kids, we walked and cycled everywhere.

We had no diesel-guzzling 4 x 4s, no electronic gadgets to charge up, no plasma tellies, no gas-fired central heating, no air-conditioning units, no projectors or computers in our classrooms, no tumble driers or dishwashers, no foreign holidays twice a year. And there was no plastic packaging on our food, no synthetic shopping bags – we walked to local shops to buy local produce, wrapped in newspaper. Soap came in un-wrapped bars, rather than out of plastic dispensers. We even recycled our glass milk bottles, which were delivered using an electric-powered vehicle called a milk float.

And yet it's always us old buggers who are made to feel guilty about destroying the planet.

I don't know how many of you have kids at home, but despite all this green indoctrination and obsession with saving the world for the next generation, I've yet to meet anybody under the age of 20 who knows how to switch off a fucking light.

Talking of which, it's time for me to switch my light off now and go to bed. I'm expecting a call from the Queen about my Damehood tomorrow. Services to science.

It'll give me a chance to pass on my condolences about Philip personally.

Nighty night.

PS: I've got a big day tomorrow. I'm going to write a suitable ending to my diary.

THE END IS NIGH:

Gentle readers, the end is nigh, so thank you for reading my secret diary, and for sticking with me this long.

Or perhaps you haven't. Perhaps you thought it was a pile of rubbish and gave up on page one, in which case you won't be reading this bit, so I can safely call you a twat.

Anyway, as lockdown gradually unwinds, I thought I'd try and summarise some of the things I've experienced over the past year or so, and put it to good use. Because, as the Government, the Police, the Local Authorities and other public bodies always insist on saying after an avoidable tragedy, 'Lessons must be learnt.'

So, these are the top 50 lessons I have learnt in lockdown, in no particular order, except possibly number order:

1. Don't buy any kitchen scrubbers from China. They're shite and they could cause a pandemic.
2. Always wash your hands, especially after turning off the tap.
3. Never trust a neighbour wielding a lump-hammer.
4. A stop-cock isn't a contraceptive.
5. Pizzas are not frisbees.
6. If you decide to grow your own tomatoes, get someone else to do it.
7. You can avoid stockpiling issues in supermarkets by getting there first.
8. Try and have your hair cut at least every two years.
9. Support bubbles can burst.
10. In tough times, flies can be very good company.

11. Identity politics is only pursued by very dull and very dangerous people.
12. It can snow in April.
13. TV adverts need to be less woke and more diverse.
14. Being Prime Minister is a shit job.
15. You can exercise without getting up.
16. Writing diaries makes the time pass quicker.
17. Reading diaries makes the time pass slower.
18. Some days, nothing at all happens.
19. If you take a home Covid test, don't post off the next-door neighbour's stool sample by mistake.
20. Helicopters are exciting if you don't have to pay.
21. Albatrosses can be lesbians.
22. Giraffes can be lesbians.
23. Swans can be lesbians.
24. Male bison often roger other male bison.
25. Female hyenas have willies.
26. The French are only interested in our fish.
27. Einstein's theory wasn't thought through properly.
28. Darwin's theory wasn't thought through properly
29. Barbara Cartland was prolific and very pink.
30. Donald Trump isn't as daft as he sounds.
31. Joe Biden is as daft as he sounds.
32. Nurses work very hard.
33. Teachers work very hard, but not very often.
34. Don't believe everything I write.
35. Nurses prefer pay rises to clapping.
36. Comedians and actors like clapping.
37. Nobody should follow a viaduct on Facebook.
38. Scientologists aren't scientists.
39. Scientists can disagree, and to prove it, they do.
40. There's no such thing as the 32nd of August.

41. Facts aren't always facts.
42. Lies are always lies.
43. Policemen shouldn't be taught at universities.
44. Clot doesn't mean the same as clit.
45. Joe Lycett is a nice Brummie.
46. Don't eat bats.
47. Jeff Bezos now has enough money ($193bn).
48. Emergency plumbers also have enough money.
49. Sorry. Can't be arsed to finish the list.
50. ………………

4th May

Just a quick update. It appears that Bill Gates is getting divorced. I reckon that's going to cost him a lot of money, so please do all you can to help by having one of his vaccines.

PTO FOR EPILOGUE

EPILOGUE:

There seems to be quite a bit of controversy in the news about Covid passports. In other words, making folk prove that they've been jabbed before they can go anywhere.

You'll remember that I referred to this in my diary entry on the 19th December last year. Here's a reminder of what I wrote then:

"Thankfully, it seems it won't be compulsory to have the jab. But if you don't have it, you can never go on a bus again, or a train, or a plane, or in a pub, or a shop. In fact, you can never leave the house again, unless it's to have the jab. And if people find out you've avoided it they'll treat you like a leper, or like someone who avoided military conscription during the war, and shoot you at dawn.

So yes, it's compulsory."

So, was I right?

Well, as I understand it, in order to put an end to all the ridiculous conspiracy theories, such as the one I hinted at on 19th December, the Government recently said it had 'no plans' to introduce Covid passports.

So, that's an end to it.

And now, to prove beyond doubt that the Government is definitely not going to introduce a Covid passport system, it's currently testing a Covid passport system.

This is because they need to test things that they are not going to introduce, just in case they introduce them, even though they're not going to.

Having tested it, they'll then say that any system they do introduce (even though they're not going to introduce one) will just be temporary. And of course the idea of making it temporary will be seen as a good compromise – especially by anyone who doesn't remember being told that there were no plans to introduce a system at all.

After all, no matter how much you might actually dislike something, making it 'temporary' always softens the blow, because it will eventually go away. Won't it? Just like Income Tax, which was introduced in 1799 as a temporary measure to help fund the Napoleonic Wars, and which the Government of the time said would be repealed as soon as the war was over.

My hot tip is…never trust a politician who uses the phrase "We have no plans to…" It usually means they intend to.

A final decision on Covid passports, as I understand it, will be made in June, and therefore probably too late for me to report about it in this diary.

Now you may, of course, be in favour of Covid passports, or you may not – I make no judgment either way.

But whichever side of the argument you're on, you've got to admit, it's a bit surprising to discover that we're still fighting the Napoleonic Wars.

"Bloody frogs," as Prince Philip might have said.

****

So, there you have it. My life tips on how to get through this unprecedented crisis. It's not been easy, and it took teamwork. I know, for example, that Doris would have struggled to get through lockdown without me. And, in turn, I occasionally also found her support useful.

Admittedly, this book may have come too late to help you with this particular crisis. I'm sorry, the timing could have been better. But please, leave it on the shelf ready for the next crisis.

Because there will be one. Or a variant of one.

You mark my words.

****

Anyway, it's been a privilege spending some quality time with you, and I hope my little diary has at least raised the occasional smile. If nothing else, you can take comfort in the fact that it has helped raise some much-needed funds for my local NHS Trust's Well Wishers charity.

And as I write that line, I suddenly realize what my 50th and final learning point of lockdown should have been.

My friends in the NHS, despite all my idle jokes to the contrary, are true working class heroes, performing a vital role in maintaining our health, in often very challenging conditions.

So, in the face of all that, I hope they'd agree with my 50th and final conclusion - that whatever life throws at you....

50. Laughter is always the best medicine.

Tarra a bit. x

Printed in Great Britain
by Amazon

42411604R00078